How Do I Begin?

SHARING YOUR FAITH

Daniel Teerman

FAITH
ALIVE®
Christian Resources

Grand Rapids, Michigan

This study is part of In the Works, a faith formation program for adults.

Studies in this series include:
Where Do I Come In? Joining God's Mission
What Do I Do with My Life? Serving God through Work
What Do I Owe? Managing the Gifts God Gives You
How Do I Make It Right? Doing Justice in a Broken World
How Do I Begin? Sharing Your Faith

Mixed Sources
Product group from well-managed forests, controlled sources and recycled wood or fiber
www.fsc.org   Cert no. SCS-COC-002464
©1996 Forest Stewardship Council

Contents

Week 4: A New Way of Thinking

Week 5: In Every Sphere

How to Use This Book

How Do I Begin? Sharing Your Faith, as well as the other books in the In the Works series, offers a unique format that combines insightful daily devotions with a discussion guide for small groups. It's simple and easy to use. Here's all you need to do:

Before your group meeting, please carefully read the five daily readings that offer insights on the topic for the week. You'll find them stimulating and full of practical ways to help you share your faith. We suggest reading one devotional on each of the five days rather than reading through all five at once. That way you can take your time and reflect on what the reading says to you personally. You may want to highlight lines that speak to you or jot questions or comments in the margin.

Note: Before your first small group session, you should have received a copy of this book so you can read the daily readings for Week 1 prior to your first meeting.

During your group meeting, use the small group discussion guides found at the end of each week of readings. These self-directing guides offer plenty to talk about for forty-five minutes to an hour or more. Groups should feel free to use them selectively, choosing the questions or activities that fit the group and the amount of time you have.

Each discussion guide includes

- an **Opening** question or activity that takes group members into the topic for the session.
- a **Bible Study** of passages that relate to the topic of the week. Group members should bring their own Bibles to the meetings or arrange to have a supply of Bibles available.
- **Group Discussion** questions that take participants back into the daily readings for the week and help relate them to their daily lives. Groups should feel free to select which of these questions they want to discuss; of course, you can

always substitute questions and comments from group members for our precooked ones!

- a brief **Closing** time of focus and prayer.
- **Action Options** for groups and for individuals. These are suggestions for follow-up activities that flow from the daily readings and group discussion.

From time to time, the discussion guides offer **Options** or **Alternative Approaches**, giving groups a choice of activities or questions.

Of course you'll want someone who's willing to lead the discussion and keep things moving for each small group meeting. But the discussion guide is written for the whole group, not just the leader. Together, may you grow in your understanding of how to begin sharing your faith in response to God's call to spread the good news.

—Faith Alive staff

Envision & Pray: If you commit, God will lead someone to himself through you! It might take weeks. It might take years. But God has done it in many Christians' lives & will do it in ours!

Introduction

*"Everyone who calls on the name of the Lord will be saved." How,
then, can they call on the one they have not believed in? And how
can they believe in the one of whom they have not heard? And how
can they hear without someone preaching to them? And how can
they preach unless they are sent? As it is written: "How beautiful
are the feet of those who bring good news!"*

—Romans 10:13-15

When I was a young boy I was terrified of being in front
of the other students in my class. I didn't know what
to do with my hands, and I was almost certain my
classmates didn't want to hear what I had to say. This fear became a paralyzing agent that seeped into my walk of faith.

Telling people about Jesus seemed more like selling outdated
encyclopedias door-to-door than sharing good news. But then
I began to consider it from another perspective. It's really the
story of how a friend of mine, who happens to be King, cleared
away all my past mistakes through his sacrifice. What's more,
this King has great plans for me as an adopted son in his kingdom. I realized that this is an exciting story worth telling. It is
a story that I *must* tell.

Some of us have been conditioned as Christians to be un-
fruitful as disciples. The way we think may need adjusting so
that our actions not only match what we say we believe, but
they become instrumental in helping us to live the most fruit-
filled lives.

Perhaps you can relate to my fear as a young boy standing in
front of the class when it comes to sharing your faith. You've
been taught that your faith is personal, even private. It's one of
the things—along with politics—our culture teaches us to keep
to ourselves. Or maybe you've just assumed that you don't have

7

a story worth sharing. You think it's boring or uneventful, and you're afraid of your life being marked as insignificant.

That leaves you in a tenuous position. You want people to get to know Jesus, you really do, but you're also secretly hoping they find him some other way that doesn't involve you. Maybe you've played this out in your mind a hundred different ways, trying to figure out how to achieve both desires: "How can these people know Jesus without me messing it up? Do I have what it takes to contribute?" Maybe you've even settled on the position that you are actually "taking one for the team" by not "messing up" someone's chance of knowing Jesus. This inner struggle is a healthy call to obedience: to be and make *or shame* disciples for the King. Experiencing fear and anxiety is normal, *c) Rom,* but it can also be a tool the enemy uses to cut down your abil- *1:16* ity to bear fruit in God's garden.

What if you could learn some skills that would help you be a more effective witness? What if you began to understand that it doesn't have to be so scary after all? What if you learned to exercise your faith muscles and engage with people in a way that didn't make you feel like the kid in front of class with sweaty palms every time?

I want to walk alongside you in this journey of discovery. All of us are people "in the works"—and we're supposed to help each other along the way. You have a story to share because the Storyteller created you. It's God's story, and God has a part for you to play in it. Let's walk together so that others can know this story and their part in it as well. Let's go!

We Begin Together

The Great Cloud

*These were all commended for their faith, yet none of them received
what had been promised. God had planned something better for us
so that only together with us would they be made perfect. Therefore,
since we are surrounded by such a great cloud of witnesses, let us
throw off everything that hinders and the sin that so easily entangles.
And let us run with perseverance the race marked out for us,
fixing our eyes on Jesus, the pioneer and perfecter of faith.*
—Hebrews 11:39-12:2a

Everything changed the day that I became a father. I began to take more seriously what I would pass on to my
children and to their children; the legacy I would leave
behind. I remember vowing that *I* would let my children stay
up late for important moments of television history—like Evel
Knieval jumping a tank of sharks with his motorcycle. I didn't
get to see that, but now I find myself imposing on my children
a bedtime discipline that is undoubtedly more important than
the crazed actions of a stunt man. Most of us have made similar
vows, promising never to say things like, "Because I said so,"

only to hear the words come out of our mouths from a place we didn't even know existed. Whether we're aware of it or not, we stand on the shoulders of those who have gone before us.

Foundational to leaving a legacy is building on the lives of those who have gone before us. Sifting through the positive and negative patterns we inherit from parents, teachers, or other significant influencers is a constant challenge. People in our lives, along with their habits, have become a part of us. What will we keep that is worth standing on, passing along to our children? What trend will we break, desperately hoping not to pass it on?

The author of Hebrews describes our spiritual ancestors, those who have gone before us, as "a great cloud of witnesses." These are the ones through whom God worked out his salvation and gave us as examples to follow, strong shoulders on which we can stand.

Some of the names in Hebrews 11 are familiar: Noah, Abraham, Isaac, Jacob, Sarah, Moses, Rahab. Countless others, unnamed, are examples of obedience to God's call in the face of seemingly ridiculous odds—jeered, flogged, stoned, sawed in two, and put to death by the sword. All of them persevered through trials "by faith"—not a faith they somehow stirred up on their own, but by desperately seeking and obeying Jesus, the "pioneer and perfecter" of faith. We are surrounded by this community of faith.

This community is informative to our witness. From them we understand, first of all, that the good news about Jesus is not a tale someone invented; it's rooted in history. The early disciples were *witnesses* to what God did through Jesus. They lived its reality. Second, their stories can comfort us in our own struggles and suffering. Peter reminds us not to be surprised at difficulties we'll encounter when living out our witness as a community: "Do not be surprised at the fiery ordeal that has come on you to test you, as though something strange were happening to you" (1 Peter 4:12). It's happened before and it will happen again. Third, we understand with much more clarity what our community of faith is supposed to look like—a community of faith, perseverance, and power. A community in which God actively partners with people who understand that their lives are part of something greater than themselves. Something worth dying for.

Consider this "great cloud"—those who have gone before us and those who will come after us—as a team working toward the same goal: to proclaim Jesus as Lord and Savior to all people for the glory of God the Father. Everyone must hear. All of us are called to play our part in this community of proclamation.

God is not limited by us, but in his infinite wisdom, he has chosen to unfold the kingdom through people working in community with each other. How will you step into this community of faith? In what way will you identify with the great cloud of witnesses and stand on their shoulders? It's time to look forward through the lens of history and evaluate the legacy you will leave, taking your place in that great cloud.

Materialism keeps us focused on work for what it can afford us, not the opportunities for witness that it affords for God. But we're a long way now from the desperate, survival mode of immigrants to the USA. God has provided. If you make over $ you're middle class. Even if not, God will provide.

Individualism keeps us distant from fellow Christians we can learn from (and be held accountable to), and distant from people God wants to make alive again with the power of the gospel.

If work is like the windshield God provides to protect us from the elements we can take our focus off the windshield of frantic work and look through our work (which still needs attention) to see the purpose God has in it for his kingdom & bringing others to faith through it.

...we need to take our eyes off the windshield while we're driving & trust God that it's there & will be, & look ahead

They Will Know . . .

"A new command I give you: Love one another. As I have loved you,
so you must love one another. By this everyone will know
that you are my disciples, if you love one another."
—*John 13:34-35*

I t was one of the last days of a much-anticipated youth group mission trip, working with the children in an orphanage in a seemingly forgotten piece of the globe. The air hung like an unwelcome guest, making T-shirts feel like soggy dishrags. It had to be pushing 100 degrees, with over 90 percent humidity. Although the morning had been successful for the most part, an underlying tension simmered among the group. The day ended with a dusty bus ride back to the campus where they were staying.

All week Jamie had interacted with the children at the orphanage with enviable skill and ease. At first the group welcomed having her "take charge." But as the week went by, the rest of the group began to feel more useless every day. They thought they'd come prepared to share the good news about

Jesus, but it was hard to connect with the kids, who were constantly being pulled into Jamie's newest "wow" project. That day it was making balloon animals. How could any of the others measure up to that?

As they rounded the corner to the campus, Jamie said, "Wasn't this the greatest day, you guys?" Someone responded, "Yeah, I'm sure it was for you. You're so awesome!" "What do you mean by that?" asked Jamie, obviously hurt.

That was all it took to blow the lid off the "negative soup" that had been simmering for days.

As group members trudged off the bus, the pitch and tone of their voices grew in intensity. It attracted the attention of several others, including their adult leader, who was preparing dinner. Then the group grew silent as they noticed the director of the orphanage standing silently nearby. She looked as though she'd been pierced from the inside. Tears slid down her cheeks. Ashamed, the young people averted their eyes, staring at the ground.

Finally, she spoke. "You came here to love the children," she began in her Caribbean accent. "And you seem to love the children well. I hear you talk of this Jesus you serve," she continued, "but if you love the children and this Jesus the way you love each other, then I don't want to know this Jesus." A look of sadness crossed her face, as if someone had taken something back that she had come to treasure, a hope that had been stolen.

At that moment, everyone knew the damage their quarrelling had caused. They'd offered the hope of the gospel and then undermined that hope by their actions. The weight of the moment crashed on them as they realized that their witness had been broken.

Our witness is a precious commodity that we throw away when we don't love each other well. At times we want to be right more than we want to be in relationship. We slip on pride and fear instead of walking the more difficult path of love.

Jesus gave us a clear lesson on loving each other well. In the middle of the disciples' monotonous debates over who was the greatest among them, Jesus wrapped a towel around his waist and began to wash his disciples' feet. He then taught them a new command: "As I have loved you, love one another."

If we do this, our witness will speak for itself.

Lord, help me to love Alicia well, so that many in our church, neighborhood, & social circles will know you.

Who's in the House?

He did not discriminate between us and them,
for he purified their hearts by faith. . . .
"It is my judgment, therefore, that we should not make
it difficult for the Gentiles who are turning to God."
—Acts 15:9, 19

I t was one of "those" churches. You know the kind I mean—a beautiful steeple and beautiful people. People were smiling, children were enfolded into a high-energy cacophony of sights and sounds, and captivating brochures were thrust into our hands offering an array of opportunities to participate in the ministries of the church. Our family was eagerly welcomed.

But I noticed a different scene unfolding across the lobby as a young couple cautiously entered through the mahogany doors. The well-dressed people with polished smiles didn't engage this couple. Beyond the antiquated rebellion of blue jeans, they sported several piercings in interesting places and had more art decorating their bodies than the Louvre. As they made their way into the building I noticed people parting, not sure how to engage them. I couldn't help wondering, "How are these people going to see Jesus today?"

I'd like to think most of us realize that it's not how we look on the outside that matters, but what's in the heart. We certainly still make assumptions and stereotype, making it more difficult to see who people really are. But it's the more subtle barriers we erect that sometimes become stumbling blocks for our witness. We have become more sophisticated in our exclusion.

Jesus hit hard on the theme of stumbling blocks on several occasions. One of the most memorable happened in the temple courts. Merchants were buying and selling in the temple court known as the Gentile court. The merchants had developed an elaborate and deceptive system to cheat people who were buying animals to sacrifice. But what stirred Jesus' righteous anger even more was *where* they were conducting this thievery: in the Gentile court. The Gentile court was the place designated for Gentiles to come and pray and worship. But the hubbub of all those merchants hawking their wares made prayer and worship impossible. It was preventing the Gentiles from coming to faith. What was worse, the people didn't care. No wonder Jesus proclaimed, "'My house will be called a house of prayer,' but you are making it a 'den of robbers'" (Matthew 21:13).

The early missionaries to the Gentiles found themselves echoing Jesus when they came before the leaders of the church in Jerusalem. The church wanted to limit the Gentiles from full participation in the church, insisting that they had to follow certain guidelines and practices in order to be fully accepted as believers. Let me say here that this desire was not considered unreasonable. This was flying in the face of hundreds of years of tradition and interpretation of how God worked through his people. It was a structure that was followed, and, until now, the pieces fit nicely.

But Peter, followed by Paul and Barnabas, testified that the Holy Spirit was doing a new thing among the Gentiles. They urged the council not to "make it difficult" for the new Gentile believers. The discussion of the council concluded fairly well, though probably not quite as well as Paul would have hoped, according to the grace that had been given him.

If we're honest, we have to admit our own tendency toward funneling people into a certain mold. It's safe. It's understandable. But the barriers we maintain can greatly diminish our witness. These may be barriers of prejudice in our hearts, or barriers in our organizational structure. Often the barriers rest in our personal expectations of others—of how they are supposed to look and act.

So let's renew our witness as the church of Jesus Christ. Instead of imposing or maintaining the barriers that make it difficult for others to belong, let's fiercely love others, trusting the Holy Spirit to do the work of purifying their hearts by faith.

Can I Get a Witness?

*"I looked for someone among them who would build up the
wall and stand before me in the gap on behalf of the land
so I would not have to destroy it, but I found no one."*
—*Ezekiel 22:30*

I play soccer in an adult recreation league. An interesting
dilemma arises before every game—who is going to play
goalie? Those who play soccer know it's a beautiful game.
Players each have their specific roles in working together toward a common goal: shooting the ball into the opponents'
net. Another key aspect of the game, as you can imagine, is to
keep your opponents from scoring. That is the key function of
the goalie: to guard the goal. Goalies may even use their hands
to stop the ball. So why is it so hard to find someone who's willing to stand in the goal?

There are several reasons. First, being a goalie can be scary.
The ball can come at the goalie quite fast, and there's little
time to react. Often a goalie must sacrifice his or her body to
protect the goal. Other times, being a goalie can be boring. A

good offense can keep the action away from the goal, leaving the goalie with little to do. Finally, being a goalie comes with tremendous pressure to perform. Games are often won or lost because of the goalie's actions. A great weight of responsibility can be crunched into a matter of milliseconds.

Being a witness to our faith in this often hostile world can have similar difficulties. Think of the church as a large team with a variety of players. We need people who are willing to stand in the gap and endure these difficulties. Sometimes being a witness can be scary; it may require us to endure mocking or perhaps worse (Hebrews 11:36-38). But take heart. Jesus tells us not to worry about how we will defend our faith or what we will say (Luke 12:11). If he places you in that situation the Holy Spirit, who lives in you (1 John 4:13) will give you the words to say.

Other times we may feel useless, unqualified, or even bored with our witness. We may wonder if we really have anything to offer. We may wonder if anyone would be interested in our story if we've grown up in the faith and can't identify a dramatic transformative moment in our lives. But whether we realize it or not, each of us has a purpose and a very precious story to tell (Psalm 139:14).

Like the pressures experienced by a goalie, being a witness sometimes creates a great weight of responsibility. But don't worry. Listen and be obedient to what you are called to do. Do your best and continue to learn from your mistakes, but leave the results to God. After all, "neither the one who plants nor the one who waters is anything, but only God, who makes things grow" (1 Corinthians 3:7). We have been given a wonderful gift to enjoy, but we have a responsibility to share this gift with others (1 Corinthians 4:1-2). Who will stand in the gap and be a witness?

Isaiah was called to a difficult task and a stubborn people. He encountered the shekinah glory of God in the temple and was undone: "Woe to me! I am ruined! For I am a man of unclean lips . . ."(Isaiah 6:5). Like Isaiah, the closer we draw to the presence of God, the more our need of God becomes apparent.

In that posture of dependence, God had Isaiah right where he needed him to be. He essentially asks Isaiah if there was anyone who would consider proclaiming a message of salvation to a difficult and stubborn people. Isaiah, having encountered the living God, realized that this was a call he dare not ignore.

"That's fine for Isaiah," you may be thinking, "and for the people God calls to be pastors and missionaries—but I'm not cut out to be one of them."

I can tell you that in the presence of God, you *are* "one of them." God chooses to work through all of his children to bring about his kingdom. Including you. It begins by answering the call of the Father: Can I get a witness? And it continues in a posture of surrender before the presence of God. God does the rest. God guides and directs the "where" and the "how" by his Spirit when we are willing to stand in the gap.

Let It Grow

*Blessed are those who do not walk in step with the wicked or stand
in the way that sinners take or sit in the company of mockers,
but who delight is in the law of the LORD and meditate on his
law day and night. They are like a tree planted by streams
of water, which yields its fruit in season and whose leaf
does not wither—whatever they do prospers.*

—Psalm 1:1-3

G rowing grapes can be difficult. It requires the right vine
stock, the right soil, and an attentive gardener. If any
one of these elements is missing, the chance of pro-
ducing good fruit is reduced significantly. Left to themselves,
vines have a natural tendency to grow deeply into the ground,
putting down roots rather than produce fruit. In order for the
vines to produce fruit, the gardener has to lift them up.

Jesus says, "I am the true vine, and my Father is the gardener.
He cuts off every branch in me that bears no fruit, while every
branch that does bear fruit he prunes so that it will be even
more fruitful" (John 15:1-3).

In this passage, Jesus identifies himself as the vine, the Father as the gardener, and God's people as the branches. To interpret the first part of the passage about "cutting off" the branches, we need to understand the role of the gardener. The gardener values the vine stock and the branches so much that cutting is a last resort to saving the vine. Instead the gardener lifts up the vine and the branches off the ground, giving them every chance to produce good fruit. The original word translated as "cuts off" is *airo*, which means "to take up." God's pruning involves a certain amount of cutting, but our Father the gardener values his children to such a degree there is significantly more lifting up and dusting off that happens before cutting ever begins.

Our hope and assurance of salvation is found in Jesus, who came to glorify his Father, the gardener, and to lift up the rest of the branches. "I, when I am lifted up from the earth, will draw all people to myself" (John 12:32). If we are in Jesus and are not bearing fruit, we must allow Jesus to lift us up and prune away whatever is getting in the way of a fruitful life—a life lived for the gardener's glory. When a gardener cares for a vine and its branches in this way, the vine will live on indefinitely.

I think this presents a rich lesson for all of us. We all have a tendency to get rooted in complacency. We'd rather burrow deep and be secure than be lifted up and exposed, let alone suffer the discomfort of being pruned. Fortunately we have a Savior who lived among us in perfect balance: rooted in the fertile soil of the gardener and lifted up in faith. Jesus' life provides a fruit-filled example we are called to follow. Our Father, the gardener, uses the soil of his Word and cultivation of the Holy Spirit through the vine of Jesus Christ to help us grow and produce good fruit.

If we're disconnected from the vine, we cannot grow and we will not produce fruit. And if we only grow inward, hiding underneath God's good soil, we'll also miss the gardener's purpose for us—to produce fruit. But when we remain connected to the vine, something amazing happens. We begin to see fruit appear all around us. This happens because of our connection, not

even if a fruitful life beckons.

because of our effort. A tree doesn't strain to grow or produce fruit—that's just what it was created to do.

The witness of the church is like that. When we are connected to the original gardener through the vine, Jesus Christ, we will be what we were created to be: a living, growing witness to the world. The Spirit produces fruit effortlessly and naturally throughout our lives as long as we stay connected to the vine.

Our witness to the world depends on it.

Discussion Guide

Opening *(10 minutes)*

Turn to a person right next to you and briefly discuss what comes to mind when you hear the word *witness*. Do you have good thoughts? Anxious thoughts? Does it conjure up notions of duty or privilege? Does it create feelings of being alone or belonging?

Then have someone read the following focus statement aloud:

God is waiting for his people to come together and be the body he sent his Son to redeem. We begin by recognizing that we're on this journey together—a journey some of us may have been walking for far too long on our own. As participants in God's story, with a history and a future, we find our strength in Jesus . . . *together*. Connecting with God and connecting with each other will bring about the unity for which Jesus prayed and will allow our witness to impact the world, through the power of the Spirit. And it all begins with a shared life.

Bible Study *(15-20 minutes)*

Read the following Scripture passages. Then use the questions below to guide your discussion.

- Hebrews 2:5-18; Romans 8:16-17
  After reading these passages, what great advantages do we have as a community of faith compared to other communities (such as clubs or other associations) you may be a part of?

- Ephesians 4:4; 1 Corinthians 12:12-27
  Reflect on how the body of Christ is supposed to function. What are some ways that you can build up the body rather than tear it down in your small group? In your neighborhood or local community? In the world? List at least three reasons why it is necessary for the body of Christ to be unified and working together.

Activity Variation
Divide into two small groups, each reading and discussing one set of passages and questions above. Leave enough time for the small groups to report to the larger group.

Discussion *(20 minutes)*

As time permits, discuss some or all of the following questions. Or discuss questions raised by group members instead.

1. "In God's infinite wisdom, he has chosen to unfold the kingdom through people working in community with each other" (Day 1). How does this partnership with God and with others encourage and shape your daily witness?

2. Reflect on a time when you felt wronged and thought you had a right to confront someone. How did it turn out? What might you have done differently? How did it either uphold the integrity of your collective witness with other Christians and your witness with non-Christians or not?

3. In what ways can our church, our "religion," our way of doing things (even good things) become stumbling blocks that get in the way of people knowing Jesus?

4. It is said that people don't understand the "why" of evangelism so they're not concerned with the "how." How is this true (or not) in your own experience? Why is being a witness so important?

5. "When we remain connected to the vine, something amazing happens. We begin to see fruit appear all around us. This happens because of our connection, not because of our effort" (Day 5). How do you stay connected to the vine, Jesus? Are there good things in your life that sometimes cause you to "burrow deep" rather than risk being exposed and "lifted up," leading to more fruit?

Alternate Approach

Instead of using the five discussion questions above, spend some time paging through the daily readings together, and have group members raise their own questions and comments about what ideas resonated with them.

Closing (5-10 minutes)

The Greek word *koinonia* refers to an intimate bond of fellowship, a sharing community that seeks to have things in common and be in agreement. Only in Christ is it possible to find unity in our diversity. Spend some time praying for the bond of fellowship to develop in your small group together as you begin this study on sharing your faith, perhaps "popcorn" style as people are led. Close your prayer by praying the Lord's prayer in unison.

Action Options

Group: Choose one of the following options for following up this session with your group:

Option 1

As a group, visit a local congregation, preferably one that's not part of your denomination. After the service, list three things you noticed that contributed positively to the body of Christ (things like teaching, hospitality, or creativity). Try to list *unique* qualities without entertaining negative qualities.

Option 2

Read Matthew 18 together and review the appropriate steps to lovingly confronting others to protect our witness as servants of Jesus. It may not always be neat; in fact, quite often it is messy, but this effort toward appropriate reconciliation honors God and promotes a witness for the world to emulate. List them on a board or sheet of newsprint, and then think of a specific situation in your community to which you could apply these steps.

Personal: Here are a couple of options for following up this session on your own this week:

Option 1

Take some time to write a list of people who helped shape your walk of faith. Pray for them one at a time. If you get a chance, call or send a note to at least one of the people on your list and thank them for allowing you to "stand on their shoulders."

Option 2

"If it is possible, as far as it depends on you, live at peace with everyone" (Romans 12:18). Make an effort to step toward peace with those whom you are not at peace. Share a phone call, a kind word, or an all-out plea for forgiveness and understanding. Protect your witness as you go through your day in what you do and what you say. Make sure there is no separation between your walk and talk.

More Than Words

The "E-word" That Makes Us Sweat

For the Spirit God gave us does not make us timid, but gives us power, love and self-discipline. So do not be ashamed of the testimony about our Lord or of me his prisoner. But join with me in suffering for the gospel, by the power of God.
—2 Timothy 1:7-8

You can find the results of a global survey of people's worst fears posted online. The survey shows that death came in at number 2. Speaking in front of people was number 1. Most people cringe at the thought of sharing their story with others; some would rather die! No wonder the idea of sharing our faith inspires more fear than fervor. Just hearing the word *evangelism* is enough to make some people begin to sweat.

It's time to dispel some of the fear associated with the "e-word"!

Even a man like Moses, raised as a prince of Egypt and undoubtedly trained in politics, leadership, and war, was afraid to stand up and speak to Pharaoh. When God called him, Moses came up with a list of excuses: I can't speak, I can't relate, I've got other stuff to do. Most of us can identify. The idea of talking to others about our faith makes us uncomfortable and fearful.

Just what is it about evangelism that causes us to react with fear and excuses? How can we reduce the anxiety that evangelism efforts cause in our life of faith? Here are a few things to consider as we *redefine* evangelism:

- *The Personality.* We typically picture an evangelist as having a "type-A," charismatic personality—someone who loves to knock on strangers' doors and chat about Jesus. This is one kind of personality and one method of evangelism, but God has created each of us with our own personality—shy or outgoing, serious or funny, introverted or extroverted. Take heart, no personality shifts or lobotomies are required to equip you to share the reason for your hope. Be yourself . . . as God has made you. *Evangelism doesn't require a personality type; it's the lifestyle of one who loves Jesus.*

- *The Conversation.* We often assume that an evangelist is someone who "has all the answers." One who can communicate God's gift of salvation with snappy illustrations and bullet points in a seamless presentation that would crack the most jaded atheist. Not true. People are more interested in connecting with someone who really cares about them than they are in listening to a smooth presentation. Often the most effective evangelists say very little and listen a lot. *Authenticity and transparency go a long way toward reaching people for Jesus.*

- *The Gift.* Some people shy away from evangelism because they don't have "the gift" of evangelism. That may be true, but it doesn't let us off the hook. We all have different gifts. Talking about our faith may come more easily to one person than the other, perhaps, in part, because we've been trying too hard to wear the skin of some preconceived notion of what an evangelist should be. Dig deeper into your relation-

34

ship with Jesus and practice sharing a sentence or two with someone about his presence in your life. Work at it. Like anything else, it gets easier and more "natural" with practice. Just don't quit. Or forget to start. *The only way to truly do evangelism wrong is to do nothing.* *Like exercising.*

As a child, I was very uncomfortable sharing my faith with others—especially in the emotionally reserved ethnic subculture of my youth. As a result, I thought I'd never be able to go into the ministry, a calling I'd felt at a young age, because I didn't have the right personality. Fortunately I was wrong. I discovered that it is God who is working in me "to will and to act in order to fulfill his good purpose" (Philippians 2:13)—regardless of my personality. All I needed to do was make myself available to God and he would shape the rest.

God took this shy, awkward kid and allowed him to speak to people around the world, even you, as you read this testimony. So don't dismiss God's calling as a witness too quickly. Live into your skin and be courageous enough to stretch it. Leave the results to God.

Merge

Always be prepared to give an answer to everyone who asks
you to give the reason for the hope that you have.
But do this with gentleness and respect. . . .

—1 Peter 3:15

"What's this guy going to do next? Great, no signal . . . thanks, buddy." Sound familiar? For freeway drivers, the art of merging seems to have taken a backseat. Merging can be a complex maneuver combining just the right momentum, awareness of your surroundings, and common courtesy. Take any of these three out of the equation and you risk frustrating other drivers, at best, or causing a crash, at worst.

Great image... Sharing our faith can be a lot like merging. We need to have momentum to engage with others, an awareness of our surroundings, and common courtesy. We'll talk about each of these elements. But unlike driving on the freeway, there is grace when we miss one of these elements. God picks us up if we crash and sends us out to try again. God wants us to learn from our mistakes and keep trying. After all, this is the work to which *God* has called us. As such, we receive all that we need to accomplish it from God.

Momentum. The tricky thing with merging is that it is harder to do if you're going too slowly. On the other hand, at higher speeds, it still takes some careful navigating to be successful. Often the first step is the most difficult part of witnessing. It's time to get moving. Begin right where you are and take that first step, trusting the Holy Spirit to give you whatever you need at this particular time, with this particular person.

Pick up speed by getting into the Word & praying (serving)

Peter tells us we should always be prepared to "give an answer" to people who want to know the reason for the hope we have. This isn't a command to prepare a polished testimony or to have all the answers. Rather, we're called to willingly share our life in Christ with others. Don't let fear hold you back or keep you from moving forward. Get moving; merge your life to bring the hope of Jesus Christ to someone else.

Awareness. Without awareness a person can have all the momentum she needs and still crash into someone. The gospels show how Jesus dealt with each person differently. With some he overturned tables and with others he spoke gently or not at all. Jesus knew who he was, but he was also acutely aware of the people he encountered—he knew their dreams and fears, their brokenness and need because he lived and walked among them.

Compassion Care

Maybe you've heard the saying "People don't care what you know until they know that you care." That's true—especially in the context of evangelism. Being involved with people and getting to know them creates awareness of how you can best reach them. There's no one-size-fits-all approach to sharing your faith. What fun would that be? Become more aware of how God has designed you to interact with others. Then let that awareness help you connect with people at their point of need, and watch beautiful friendships emerge as a result of your obedience.

Courtesy. Peter's words *gentleness and respect* also apply here. Some drivers can execute a merge, perhaps even skillfully, but

Members will care for others when they sense care from their pastor, too. eachother and

they seem to have an element of unconcern for those sharing the roadway. Jesus took great care to present the good news of the kingdom, but he didn't force anyone to follow him. He invited. Jesus still invites people today with gentleness and respect: "Here I am! I stand at the door and knock" (Revelation 3:20). In our zeal to win people to Jesus, let's remember that they are people and not products of our piety. Be patient and walk in step with the Spirit. You'll find that it's more fun that way, and you'll gain a friend.

As I'm driving the freeway, I don't have to think much about the elements of merging anymore. It just comes naturally. The same will be true the more you engage others with your faith—sometimes by sharing a story, other times in prayer, but often simply by listening, which can be the most profound witness of all. Jesus never intended for evangelism to be goofy or awkward. Keep "merging" and it will soon become an everyday part of your journey as you walk with him.

Talk Is Cheap

Do not merely listen to the word, and so
deceive yourselves. Do what it says.

—*James 1:22*

I travel quite often. So I get to spend time in some of the worst places on the planet: airports. I don't mind flying— who can beat the experience of shoving as many people into the smallest space possible and then launching into the air? But I digress. With all the delays and empty promises— "We're overbooked but we'll get you on the next flight"—the airport can be a place of perpetual frustration.

The point of an airport is to get people moving to another destination, not just talk about doing so. When the airport functions the way it was designed to function, all is well. When it does not—when the weary traveler hears a voice over the intercom announcing yet another "ten-minute delay" (more often code for an hour), people end up frustrated. Talk is cheap. *Or simply "I'll be home in 15 minutes."*

If you've been to an airport, you've experienced this. After about the third "delay" you begin to smell that there was

39

something the airline knew would take longer right from the start. Talk is cheap.

What does this have to do with evangelism? Sometimes we find ourselves *talking* more about witnessing than actually *doing* it. We can place so much energy into outreach planning and programs that we forget that our main purpose is to launch the aircraft. Or we work ourselves into such a frenzy about how to evangelize that we become paralyzed and don't do it.

Have we forgotten that the church is not the destination? It is a vehicle through which we *find* the destination (or in which the destination finds us). A launching point from which people step into the world as witnesses for Jesus. The destination is the kingdom of heaven—an eternal kingdom that God desires to usher from heaven down to earth. We have the profound honor of being a conduit of this kingdom, part of an airport of sorts through which God's Spirit dwells and directs others to seek their *real* destination. As recipients of God's Spirit we are instructed to be "doers of the Word" and not just "hearers," to be the church and not just talk about it. Talk is cheap.

Jesus identified this trap too: "Why do you call me 'Lord, Lord' and do not do what I say?" he said (Luke 6:46). This seemed ridiculous to Jesus, especially in Hebrew culture where hearing and the act of obeying were so closely tied that they were expressed with one word—*shema.* A person didn't really know something until it was reflected in his or her life, and Jesus' listeners had not really taken what he said to heart until their lives were demonstrating transformation.

It's like building a house on the ground without a foundation, said Jesus. Without a foundation of action, words fall apart. They simply cannot stand on their own. Jesus wants his followers not just to talk about his message, not simply theorize or evaluate what he says, but to put his words into practice.

We need to be convicted of this too. It's too easy for us to hear a message from God's Word, and then go home and evaluate the profundity and excellence of what was said without turning it into action. Talk is cheap.

Talk is cheap without the actions that support it. Jesus makes that clear. On the other hand, when we combine our words with a genuine concern for the needs of others, we demonstrate the fullness of the gospel living through us as God intended.

Start a Twitter account to get people talking about their witnessing.

True Religion

Religion that God our Father accepts as pure and faultless is this:
to look after orphans and widows in their distress
and to keep oneself from being polluted by the world.

—James 1:27

saw the open wound of God's heart in Africa. I saw an eighty-seven-year-old grandmother left to care for her nine grandchildren because her ten children died of AIDS. I saw a little girl digging in the dirt to find roots to fill her grumbling stomach. I saw a look of desperation and hopelessness in the eyes of children too young to know that kind of pain.

I also saw hope firsthand in Africa. Hope in the thankful voices of 167 orphans singing at the top of their lungs how blessed they felt to have food, teachers, and visitors. Hope in homes filled with orphans instead of "empty nesters." Hope in the eyes of a man who dreams of overcoming more than physical poverty for his people. Hope in the relationships of people bearing each other's burdens.

Hope can be believed individually but it can only be lived out in community. The people I met in Africa know what it means to live out this hope as they cling to the promises of Jesus even as they struggle with the daily grind of poverty.

How is God calling us to meet the needs of people like these and countless others around the world? It's not a question of *if* God is calling, but *how*. I believe our response must begin and end with the gospel of Jesus.

For centuries there has been a wrestling match between proponents of a social, liberal gospel and an evangelistic, conservative gospel. Which communicates the gospel of Jesus most effectively? I believe both do, as measured and directed by the Holy Spirit. At times the pendulum has swung in the direction of "social" gospel—caring for people's physical, social, and emotional needs, working with people to develop enough food, clean water, education, and the other things people need in order to thrive. Christians must be on the front lines of these efforts.

Other times the pendulum has swung in the direction of "evangelistic" gospel—proclaiming the message of the gospel as the first priority. After all, Jesus said, "What good will it be for you to gain the whole world, yet forfeit your soul?" (Matthew 16:26). I believe Jesus' hyperbole here gives us pause to recognize the high priority of presenting something of eternal value, intrinsically greater than temporary needs. We cannot neglect proclaiming the good news, hoping that our social action alone will plant the seed of the gospel in people's hearts (Romans 10:14; Acts 8:31).

In our culture it is more acceptable to help people with their social needs. Governments around the world welcome relief workers with open arms, not caring what they believe or the motivation behind their action. It is far more difficult to present Jesus as the answer to spiritual poverty in these same circles. Christ-followers who proclaim this message are persecuted around the world, but we rarely hear of people persecuted for giving bread and clean water to those in need. That's humanity. Our humanity necessitates a proclamation that is rooted outside ourselves and administered by the Holy Spirit to penetrate lives for eternal transformation.

Moses and Jesus said that there will always be poor people among us (Deuteronomy 15:11; Mark 14:7). How we respond to the needs of the poor will depend on how we define poverty. Do we recognize only physical or social poverty, or can we also see a deeper spiritual poverty that needs to be healed by the Spirit's power? Do we have the courage to love people completely: with physical bread in one hand and the Bread of Life in another?

The Great Commission and the Great Commandment call us to go into the world, teaching others the ways of Jesus and loving our neighbor as ourselves (Matthew 28:18-20; Luke 10:27). True religion in word and deed.

The Art of Listening

Then Jesus said, "Whoever has ears to hear, let them hear."
—*Mark 4:9*

I met Bob in an airport as I stood in line to get a sandwich. Bob was a traveling executive who believed in Jesus. In fact, that was the first thing he said to me. I told him I was a believer as well. Bob didn't hear me. I'd barely had a chance to admire his boldness before the grilling began: "Do you know that you need to repent to have your sins forgiven? Jesus is coming back any day and you must be ready." "Um, yes," I replied. "I have trusted Jesus as my Lord and—" Bob cut in, "Because if you don't, you'll spend eternity in hell." At this point I wasn't sure if the sandwich was worth it.

Bob continued to hammer me with the four spiritual laws and every other evangelistic tool designed since Moses walked the earth. I couldn't get a word in edgewise to let him know he'd "made the sale." He was obviously driven by something other than a genuine interest in me as a person. What troubled me most was not Bob's obnoxious personality but his inability to *listen*. Listening is a necessity for anyone who wants to lead someone to Jesus.

Jesus often spoke about the kingdom of God in parables so that people would hear and understand by faith. Seeking was required. Digging was necessary. But Jesus also *listened* for parables. Jesus listened to people's stories and uncovered hidden truths in them. He knew that as people made in the image of God, they were designed for freedom but trapped in their sin. He inspired faith by listening, seeking, and believing that their stories were connected with God's plan, even when they couldn't see it themselves.

One of the greatest examples of Jesus *listening* for parables was the Samaritan woman at the well in the book of John. When you read the story (John 4), it's easy to conclude that Jesus already knew everything about this woman and so had an "unfair" advantage over her. But I believe that in this encounter, Jesus modeled attentive listening. By listening and asking questions, Jesus intentionally and skillfully touched on the parts of the woman's story that needed to be uncovered. At first she tried to get Jesus off track from the real issues of her heart. But Jesus' loving, patient, persistent listening resulted in the woman's transformation at the deepest level. Jesus listened to her story and believed she could experience healing. He cared more about the woman than about what she thought of him. As a result of their encounter, she believed.

Listening in faith applies not only to how we hear and believe but also to how we hear others and lead them to belief. As James said, we must be "quick to listen" and "slow to speak" (1:19). *How* we listen is the key. We must listen *in faith*, looking beyond what we see to what's underneath. Seeing beneath each other's masks can be difficult, but that is where *loving people to Jesus* begins.

Our listening also directs the next steps of our witness. Where do we begin to tell someone the good news we have to share? Philip the evangelist gives us a clue: begin where the person is.

[handwritten margin note: This day/week, practice asking questions of the people you meet.]

Philip demonstrates this to perfection. The Ethiopian was sitting in his chariot, reading Isaiah with a bewildered look on his face. Philip was patiently running alongside, just waiting for the Holy Spirit to open the door. He asked the Ethiopian, "Do you understand what you're reading?" No, said the Ethiopian. Can you help me understand? (Acts 8:31). So Philip hops into the chariot. Does he turn to Genesis 1? No, Philip "began with that very passage of Scripture and told him the good news about Jesus" (Acts 8:35). Isn't that cool? He never would have known where to start or how to meet the pressing questions of the seeking Ethiopian if he hadn't been listening.

That's the key to our witnessing too. Listen, and let the Spirit do the rest.

Many of us love 'people watching'. What about 'people hearing'?

Discussion Guide

Opening *(10 minutes)*

Take turns briefly mentioning one thing from the readings this week that convicted you regarding the importance of our actions. If possible, share an example of a person you've encountered (either personally or someone you have read about or know of) who lived out what they said, more often than not.

Then have someone read the following focus statement out loud:

As a community of believers in Jesus we are called to "live out" the good news of the kingdom with our actions, serving as God's hands and feet to the world. The good news we proclaim is more than words, more than a way to make ourselves and others feel better. When we live out the good news by our actions, God uses us as agents of transformation to bring about his kingdom. Matching our actions with our words, as Jesus taught us to do, is an integral part of our witness. It's the way we live out "the reason for our hope."

Bible Study *(20 minutes)*

These first two Scripture passages can be categorized as "Let us *not*s." Read the passages, and then use the questions provided to guide your discussion.

- Hebrews 10:24-25
  Last week we focused on our witness together. How is "meeting together" an action that demonstrates our witness for Jesus?

- 1 John 3:18
  What is the difference between loving "with words" and loving "with actions and in truth"?

The second part of our study focuses on more examples of the action of our witness. Read the passages below and use the questions to guide your discussion.

- Acts 2:44-47; Acts 4:32-35
  Believers in the early church sold their possessions and shared their money "as everyone had need." This was a beautiful but extreme action. How does this relate to the Old Testament practice of tithing? Is this a new and greater action of faith for kingdom living?

  It seems clear from Acts 4:32-35 that this principle continued at least beyond the initial days of Pentecost. Do you think this is still a guiding principle for our lives today? What would it look like if the church today acted like the Acts 2:45 church?

- Acts 6:1-7
  How does the early church continue to demonstrate by example the principle of acting out its witness? What are some examples of this in our own church?

Discussion *(15-20 minutes)*

1. "The Spirit God gave us does not make us timid, but gives us power, love and self-discipline" (2 Timothy 1:7). In what ways are you living out of this kind of spirit? How does this measure with the way you are sharing "the hope that is within you"?

2. Reflect on a time when someone gave you some kind of sales pitch that made you feel uncomfortable. What was the greatest source of discomfort? Did you feel valued? Listened to? How could you apply the lessons learned from this negative experience to sharing "the hope that you have" in a positive way?

3. People who have the Spirit living inside of them sometimes experience a righteous discontentment: wanting to take more action with their faith but not quite sure how. Think of some ways you can show others that the Word of God has penetrated your heart and life. Why is it so important to show others that your witness is more than words?

4. Our witness has to include more than a tangible expression of our faith in order to love people completely. If we are serving others out of genuine concern for their need, how do we also share the reason for our hope in an equally genuine way, without coming across as having an "ulterior motive"?

5. What are some of the barriers that sometimes get in the way of our ability to listen? How is being a better witness for Jesus connected to being a better listener?

Alternate Approach
Instead of using the discussion questions above, spend some time paging through the daily readings for this week. Invite people to share their responses to the reading and to bring up their own questions.

Closing *(5-10 minutes)*

Francis of Assisi said, "Preach the gospel at all times—if necessary, use words." How can we preach the gospel with our actions? Spend a few brainstorming ideas about this. Then share any joys or concerns the group would like to pray for. Close with prayer, asking the Spirit to reveal how you can play an active role as a witness of his love and rule in a lost and broken world.

Alternate Approach

Instead of praying as a group, form pairs and share any joys or concerns each person would like to pray for. Then find a quiet space and pray together, asking the Holy Spirit to give you an opportunity to actively demonstrate God's love beyond words to someone crossing your path this week.

Action Options

Group: Line up an opportunity to serve with your group. This could be anything from connecting with a local ministry that is in need of volunteers on a Saturday, or a family on your block that could use help around their home. Make the phone call today. Don't procrastinate! Others need to see and feel your witness more than words.

Personal: Many people plan what they are going to do by writing out "to do" lists. Often our motivation is tied to necessity: we need food so we go out and buy groceries. What about your witness—do you also see living out your faith as a necessity? What would happen if you decided to "opt out" of witnessing? Come up with a list of reasons why the actions connected with your witness are necessary.

You're Not Alone

Ambassadors of Jesus

"Now get up and stand on your feet. I have appeared to
you to appoint you as a servant and as a witness of
what you have seen and will see of me."

—*Acts 26:16*

've always thought the concept of an embassy is an interesting one—having nations around the world with sovereign representation in another country. Embassies represent their nations abroad to such a degree that the building and grounds on which they stand are actually the sovereign property of the nations they represent.

The United States has embassies planted around the world. They have become havens of safety for United States citizens because they represent the ideals and freedoms of the nation. Wherever they are, they are considered a facsimile of the United States in every way. When you step through the gates of an American embassy, you are on American soil.

What is also interesting is that although embassies function in every way as United States property, the ambassadors who work and run them are citizens empowered by their government to represent their country in a foreign land. Without the acknowledgment and support of their government, ambassadors have no power or purpose.

Jesus calls us to be his ambassadors, to represent him and his kingdom in the world: "You will be my witnesses in Jerusalem, and in all Judea and Samaria, and to the ends of the earth" (Acts 1:8). As sons and daughters of the King, we are to live for his purposes, connected to his power. We are to proclaim and demonstrate Jesus' sovereign rule throughout the earth. God's "embassies" are established through believing communities, and the gates of hell will not prevail against them. As his ambassadors, we have Jesus' full support and favor. Without this, our identity is lost, our power is gone, and we are easily absorbed into the fleeting purposes of the world.

John the Baptist understood more than most what it means to be an ambassador for Jesus. "He came as a witness to testify concerning that light, so that through him all might believe. He himself was not the light; he came only as a witness to the light" (John 1:7-8). John understood that his purpose was to give witness to the original, Jesus. He knew Jesus and stayed connected to him. John experienced with his eyes, his ears, and his heart the person and work of Jesus. The apostle John knew about the role of ambassador too. He testifies: "That which was from the beginning, which we have heard, which we have seen with our eyes, which we have looked at and our hands have touched—this we proclaim concerning the Word of life" (1 John 1:1).

Even though we are not eyewitnesses, we are still credible ambassadors. Even though proximity and time separate us from Jesus' ministry on earth (as recorded in Scripture), we can testify about what we have seen and heard because Jesus *is* alive, "the same yesterday and today and forever" (Hebrews 13:8). We can believe that the historical accounts of Jesus' life and ministry are true, but more than this, the Holy Spirit affirms this truth in our hearts, making us reliable witnesses. As his witnesses we need to *know* that the life and message of Jesus are true and reliable. We must *believe* that knowing him will bring about a transformation only God can bring.

If then we are to be ambassadors of Jesus, how are we to truly *know* him? We can only represent him as much as we know him, right? Moses spoke to God face to face, "as one speaks to a friend" (Exodus 33:11). He asked, "Teach me your *ways* so I may know you" (v. 13). Moses knew that we get to know God when we discover God's ways. We get to know God's ways by observing how God acts. As we learn from God's Word and Spirit, we discover that God keeps promises. God's character is reliable, and his ways are for our good. Many of God's ways are too wonderful and lofty for us to contemplate and understand (Psalm 40:5; Isaiah 55:8-9), but God came down and made himself known to us through Jesus, "the *way* and the truth and the life" (John 14:6). God sent Jesus to live among us as an ambassador of the Father.

So if you want to know the *ways* and character of God, look to Jesus. If you want to know the will of God, look to Jesus. He is *the* original. He acted as an ambassador of the Father so that we might know the Father and let what we know shine before others (John 17:18; Matthew 5:16). When we *know* this personally, we grow as his ambassadors and believe that transformation is not only possible, it is guaranteed. When we become eyewitnesses of his majesty, everything changes and we cannot help but tell others about the One we serve.

Let the Wind Blow

"Even now my witness is in heaven; my advocate is on high. My intercessor is my friend as my eyes pour out tears to God; on behalf of a human being he pleads with God as one pleads for a friend."
—*Job 16:19-21*

I t was the day before my wedding. The sun was shining and a gentle breeze was blowing from the west. We were having a picnic with friends and family when the breeze became a little stronger. Paper plates sailed off the tables, sending potato salad in unexpected directions. As the sky grew darker more people started to head inside. I grabbed my infant nephew and turned toward the house when a great gust of wind came and swirled around us, filling the air with debris. I was struck in the forehead by a potato chip. It drew blood. Bizarre, you say? Definitely! Who's ever been cut by a potato chip?

Thinking of that mini-twister always reminds me of Pentecost. What a bizarre experience that must have been as well— the loud roar of a violent wind resulting in still, small flames of fire resting on peoples' heads! This Pentecost "wind" was no product of nature; instead, it was a "super nature" sign that the Holy Spirit had arrived to give us the *presence, power,* and *purpose* of our witness.

Jesus had told his anxious disciples that he had to leave in order for the Holy Spirit to come (John 16:7). He promised to send an Advocate "to help [them] and be with [them] forever" (John 14:16). His presence would remain with them but in a different way: "always, to the very end of the age" (Matthew 28:20). At Pentecost, the person of the Holy Spirit would come to dwell among us and even *in* us—God's presence taking up permanent residence in us.

God's Word shows us that the Holy Spirit was present from the very beginning, even before creation: "The Spirit of God was hovering over the waters" (Genesis 1:2). This same Spirit gives life and breath to every element of creation. And at Pentecost the Spirit comes to live in our hearts, bringing his comfort and power.

The power of the wind transforms calm water into waves and bends the branches of mighty trees. Likewise, the power of the Holy Spirit moves in our hearts, bringing transformation, healing, and deliverance. The good news about Jesus is not merely wishful thinking. It is a power that changes us and those we encounter. This is at the core of the Holy Spirit's purpose.

Trying to define something you cannot see is difficult. Take the color green, for instance. How would you describe it to someone who has never been able to see? In some ways, the Holy Spirit is just as hard to pin down. In his discussion with Nicodemus, Jesus describes the Spirit as blowing "wherever it pleases" (John 3:8). We can never fully understand how the Holy Spirit works, but we can look at the transformation left in the Spirit's wake. This evidence gives us reason to claim what we cannot see and to receive in faith our alignment with God's purpose. Witnessing to the good news, the apostle Paul says, "I speak the truth in Christ—I am not lying, my conscience confirms it in the Holy Spirit" (Romans 9:1). The presence of the Holy Spirit in our hearts enables Jesus to carry out his purpose in our lives.

How does the Spirit do this?

- By breaking down the sinful barriers that keep us from God (Romans 8:10).

- By teaching us what to say. Often our witness suffers because we're afraid. The Holy Spirit speaks for us and teaches us what to say (Mark 13:11; Luke 12:12).

- By helping us in our weakness. When we do not know what we ought to pray for, the Spirit himself intercedes for us "through wordless groans" (Romans 8:26).

God has chosen to work through us by the power of the Holy Spirit. But the results of our witness are up to God. We won't always know how much our actions have affected someone's decision to follow Jesus. And that's OK. Our calling is to proclaim and live out what we know is true. Period. The rest we leave in the hands of the Father.

Through the Spirit's presence we have the person of Jesus; in the Spirit's power we have every gift and possibility available to carry out his work; and in the Spirit's purpose our lives find meaning and direction, to the glory of God. So unfurl your sails and let "the wind" blow in your life.

Two by Two

Though one may be overpowered, two can defend themselves.
A cord of three strands is not quickly broken.
—*Ecclesiastes 4:12*

The Lone Ranger and Tonto. Batman and Robin. These are some of the dynamic duos who have carried the banner of companionship and partnership in our culture. This "two by two" concept has been around for a long time. God escorted the animals into the ark two by two, and Jesus sent out his disciples two by two. Why does this pattern seem to be woven into the fabric of creation? What's so significant about *two*?

It began in the garden with Adam. As the animals paraded before him to be named, he discovered that not one of them was suitable to be his partner. God took a good look and said, "It is not good for the man to be alone" (Genesis 2:18). Adam wasn't meant to enjoy perfection alone. Human beings were created for partnership.

This partnership can take on many forms. Often God brings people into our lives to walk with. Paul had Barnabas, the "son of encouragement"; later, he sat in prison with Silas. Moses had Joshua, his trusted aid. Scripture includes numerous examples that bear out our need for brothers and sisters in Christ. We need people who can sharpen our witness—sometimes by being the "mirror" we look into, pointing out the need to reshape our character; other times by offering a shoulder to cry on when the going is especially tough. But the greatest partnership we have is with One who "sticks closer than a brother" (Proverbs 18:24). A partnership with God himself.

First Corinthians 6:19 talks about this close partnership with God: "Do you not know that your bodies are temples of the Holy Spirit, who is in you, whom you have received from God? You are not your own." When we receive Jesus, he becomes our partner through the person of the Holy Spirit. We are his temple, the place where the living God, who is Creator of all things, lives.

God walks beside us just like the lead ox in a pair of oxen pulling a load. Jesus identifies with this metaphor when he says, "My yoke is easy and my burden is light" (Matthew 11:30). In other words, "My partnership is a good one. I will get you where you need to go. It won't always be an easy road, but in my strength we can handle it together."

In this partnership we can rest securely. We are free to discover the joys and challenges that come our way in partnership with the One who invites us to "love him and enjoy him forever" (Westminster Confession). Part of "enjoying God" is accepting the *partnership* he offers to love the world he created and redeemed. We are to be witnesses of Jesus' sufferings and glory because we're on his team. This is our high honor and privilege.

Peter testifies as "a witness of Christ's sufferings who also will share in the glory to be revealed" (1 Peter 5:1). Rejoice when you participate in Christ's sufferings, he says, "so that you may be overjoyed when his glory is revealed" (1 Peter 4:13). Peter knew that his life as a disciple of Jesus would not be easy (John 21). But he also knew that this was the best partnership he could ever have (John 6:68); one that was necessary to live out God's purpose for his life. The apostle Paul also recognized this when he said, "I consider that our present sufferings are not worth comparing with the glory that will be revealed in us" (Romans 8:18). God does not intend for us to witness on our own.

Partners are meant to encourage us and hopefully provide what we don't have. They complement us. God is asking us to be partners with one another, to "carry each other's burdens, and in this way . . . fulfill the law of Christ" (Galatians 6:2). But he doesn't ask us to do something that he is unwilling to do himself. God offers to be partners with us, just as we are partners with others.

Accept God's offer of partnership and join his witness to the world. While you're at it . . . bring a friend.

Sticky Gifts

This salvation, which was first announced by the Lord, was confirmed to us by those who heard him. God also testified to it by signs, wonders and various miracles, and by gifts of the Holy Spirit distributed according to his will.

—Hebrews 2:3-4

Each of you should use whatever gift you have received to serve others, as faithful stewards of God's grace in its various forms.

—1 Peter 4:10

Even after revelations of failure in his personal life, Tiger Woods was still considered the best golfer in the world. On his worst day he could beat me with one hand tied behind his back. I'm not trying to be self-deprecating—it's simply a fact. If I worked every day, all day, for the rest of my life, I still would not compare to the skill level of Tiger Woods if he never practiced again. He has very clear and specific "sticky gifts" when it comes to golf. This natural talent is a part of who he is and cannot be changed. It's part of what makes him the best golfer in the world.

Whether we realize it or not, we all have "sticky gifts." All of us are born with a natural ability to do something well. We don't have to work as hard at that certain something as others do. But that doesn't mean we shouldn't work hard at developing our "sticky gifts." In fact, those are the very things we should work to develop while managing our weaknesses.

The way we are gifted has a lot to do with what is expected of us. That is why God gives us a set of natural gifts and a set of spiritual gifts—the gifts of the Spirit. We're born with one set and we receive the other. "Flesh gives birth to flesh," said Jesus, "but the Spirit gives birth to spirit" (John 3:6). Sometimes these gifts are interwoven and other times not. But when the Creator who made us with innate natural gifts gives us spiritual gifts, these can be the stickiest of all.

The gifts of the Spirit are very specific to accomplish the work God has prepared in advance for us to do (Ephesians 2:10). All together, these gifts comprise the kingdom firing on all cylinders—being the body of Christ as God intended. Paul talks about these gifts frequently in his letters to the churches, noting that there are "different kinds of gifts, but the same Spirit" (1 Corinthians 12:4) so that the body of Christ may be built up "until we all reach unity in the faith . . . and become mature, attaining to the whole measure of the fullness of Christ" (Ephesians 4:13). Jesus has given us his presence, his power, his purpose, and the gifts of his Spirit to bring about spiritual transformation.

When we receive the Holy Spirit, we are given a unique set of "sticky gifts"—beginning with the gift of salvation. Salvation is more than an eternal ticket we can cash in on our deathbeds; it is a gift we unfold "with fear and trembling" (Philippians 2:12), using the spiritual tools we have been given. These sticky gifts are irrevocable. We might not use them, but we cannot get rid of them and are responsible for them.

Jesus talked about this in the parable of the man who entrusted his property to some servants before going on a journey (Matthew 25). To one servant he gave five bags of gold, to another two bags, and to a third, one bag. The servants with the five and two bags of gold doubled what they had, while the servant with one bag buried it. When the master came back and called on his servants to account, the servants with five and two bags of gold were praised for their work. But the servant who buried his one bag was reprimanded. The one bag of gold he had was given to the servants who developed and multiplied their master's property. This story can be applied to what God has entrusted to us, whether it be gifts of time, talent, or treasure.

Hopefully our "sticky gifts" are refined and developed as we grow into the new creation God has willed us to be. "Sticky gifts" are intended bring God glory and bless others in a transformative way, pointing people to Jesus so they too receive their "sticky gifts" from the Holy Spirit and are transformed to bless the world.

Because You Say So

Do you not know? Have you not heard? The LORD is the everlasting God, the Creator of the ends of the earth. He will not grow tired or weary, and his understanding no one can fathom.
—Isaiah 40:28

Let us not become weary in doing good, for at the proper time we will reap a harvest if we do not give up.
—Galatians 6:9

My friend Shane is a fisherman. He has a sixth sense about where to find the fish, what equipment to use, and, most importantly, how to gauge the weather. But sometimes the sixth sense starts "pinging" a little too late. This was one of those times.

The day began with a flourish of color across the horizon, promising calm seas and large catches. This held true through the late afternoon; the "well" was brimming with giant small-mouth bass. But as the sun began its final descent into the water, ominous clouds collected in the east. The rods continued to bend well after the light was gone. And then it got darker.

Aside from the flashlight, no light penetrated from shore, sky, or sea.

It was time to get going. After a final cast, Shane started the engine and fired up the GPS. Then the flashlight began to grow dim and the GPS started flickering. Twenty miles from shore in the pitch dark was not a good time to lose direction. Would the batteries last?

After the flashlight cast its last beam, the only light came from the flickering GPS. Shane had to make a decision: either stay put and ride out the storm in the dark, risking a fatal collision, or race home at high speed against the battery life of the GPS.

Shane hammered the engine to full throttle, skimming along in the darkness at well over 60 m.p.h. Not bothering to look ahead and concentrating fully on the GPS, Shane began turning the GPS on and off for periods in order to save the battery, getting a directional bearing and then shutting it down. Against every impulse to slow down, Shane put his trust solely in the GPS and his ability to follow it as fast as the boat would go.

Jesus' disciples had been out all night. They were fishermen. They knew where to find fish and when to find the best catch. They were attuned to the weather. After a fruitless night of fishing, they were headed back to shore. Then Jesus called out an audacious suggestion: "Throw your nets out on the other side!" A rabbi giving advice to professional fishermen? Peter initially resists the idea, but his secondary response is priceless: "*Because you say so*, I will let down the nets" (Luke 5:5). That's obedience: when your head tells you, "This isn't going to work," but you do it anyway. Even when you're tired.

There are times when we get tired. Tired of being tempted, tired of serving, tired of living up to expectations. This is normal, but our deepest weariness comes from a lack of trust. When we trust only in what we know we quickly become tired. Our reliance on what we can see is a sure recipe for weariness. The mystery of "when I am weak, then I am strong" (2 Corinthians 12:10) is found in the strong salvation of Jesus. He provides a way out so that we can endure temptation (1 Corinthians

10:13). By his Spirit, he gives us stamina to persevere as his witnesses (2 Thessalonians 3:5). His words are a strong tower for us to lean on when he calls us to do something we hadn't planned on.

Shane made it to the harbor safely by keeping his focus on the one thing that could get him home. Jesus calls us to focus on him—especially when we struggle. He will light the way. In times of weariness and darkness, you can trust that Jesus is pointing you in the right direction by his Word and Spirit. In our own strength we falter, in our weakness we find his strength.

Discussion Guide

Opening *(5-10 minutes)*

Think of something you did "the hard way" for a long time. Then take turns briefly describing the moment of discovery when you realized a new, easier way. (For me it was asking for directions before I reach the "thirty-minute mark" of being lost. Swallowing a little pride is much easier than wasting that much time!)

Then have someone read the following focus statement out loud:

When you receive Jesus into your heart, you are given a re-markable gift, the very presence of Jesus living in us in the person of the Holy Spirit. From this point on we receive other gifts from the Holy Spirit: spiritual gifts, direction, comfort, and power. Our natural tendency is to resist God's gifts. If we disconnect ourselves from the power and presence of the Spirit, we will experience loneliness and despair. But with the Holy Spirit living in us, we are never alone. We are em-powered to live out our faith as a witness for the One who saved us, to share the reason for our hope with others. This is a life of victory.

Bible Study *(20 minutes)*

Read the following passage, and then answer the questions below.

- James 1:17
  What does it mean to you that God's gifts are
  - ○ "good and perfect"?
  - ○ "from above"—that is, from heaven and not earth?
  - ○ from "the Father of the heavenly lights"?

What does it mean to you that this Father "does not change"—that he is steady and faithful?

Sometimes we wonder if we've received God's gifts. But all we need to do is ask! We have a generous heavenly Father (Matthew 7:11; Luke 11:13). These gifts are evidence of the Holy Spirit in our hearts, and they are irrevocable (Romans 11:29). Read the following passages and write down examples of people with the gifts listed in the Scripture passages below. Don't forget to include yourself!

- Romans 12:4-8

- 1 Corinthians 12

- Ephesians 4:1-16

Discussion *(20 minutes)*

1. As ambassadors of Jesus, we are extensions of him, "no longer slaves, but God's children . . . and also heirs" (Galatians 4:7). What does this connection mean to you? How will you make this connection to Jesus your identity, your power, and your purpose?

2. "Through the Spirit's presence we have the person of Jesus; in the Spirit's power we have every gift and possibility available to carry out his work; and in the Spirit's purpose our lives find meaning and direction, to the glory of God." How is the Holy Spirit's power evident in your life and ministry?

3. "We always carry around in our body the death of Jesus, so that the life of Jesus may also be revealed in our body" (2 Corinthians 4:10). In what ways are you a partner with Jesus in death and in life?

4. What are some of the "sticky gifts" God has given you? If you're not sure, what steps can you take to identify and use these gifts more purposefully?

5. Jesus wants to be the One we trust as our Savior, especially when we're tired, weary, and desperate. Think of such a

situation in your life. What made you able to trust God even during that dark time?

Closing *(5-10 minutes)*

Spend a few minutes sharing joys and concerns that have come up in group members' lives this past week that they would like to pray about. Then pray together in whatever style your group prefers. End your time of prayer by reading the following prayer in unison:

> Gracious Father, your generosity is like an ever-flowing stream in our lives. You're like an attentive host who continues to give more than we need. Our cups are overflowing and our platters are heaping with goodness. Forgive us when we fail to open and develop your gifts because we're afraid that your plan for our lives is beyond our control. Thank you for giving us everything we need to know you and to make you known to others. Thank you for your promise to never leave us or turn your back on us, to never leave us alone. Help us to walk with you and to invite the broken, the lonely, the desperate, and the lost to walk alongside us and open the beautiful gifts you are longing to give. Amen.

Action Options

Group: Invite someone—perhaps your pastor or someone else from your church—to come in and do a "spiritual gifts assessment" with the members of your group. This may help group members affirm some areas of giftedness and discover new areas. Even if you've already done this, new gifts can emerge as we mature spiritually and age physically. Be sure to spend some time sharing your top gifts with each other, affirming and encouraging each other to continue to develop and use these gifts in the service of God's kingdom. (An online gifts survey is available in the *Discover Your Gifts* course, available from Faith Alive, www.faithaliveresources.org.)

Personal: Buy a gift for someone today and give it with a note offering your friendship and reminding them that they're not alone; God is with them and so are you. If possible, note a gift of God you have recognized in the person's life and tell him or her how others have been blessed as a result.

A New Way of Thinking

Old Way, New Day

*And we also thank God continually because, when you
received the word of God, which you heard from us, you
accepted it not as a human word, but as it actually is,
the word of God, which is indeed at work in you who believe.*
—*1 Thessalonians 2:13*

Salaam awoke from the dream with a start, drenched in sweat. He was a Muslim living in Iraq. And yet the message had been clear. In the dream Jesus and had said, "Salaam, I love you and I am asking you to follow me." How could this be? Salaam tossed and turned the rest of the night. What would he tell his wife, Miriam? If it became known that he was a follower of Jesus, she would desert him and perhaps tell the leaders of the village. Salaam knew what that meant, and it made him shiver. Why did Jesus come to him, and how was he supposed to follow him in a place where everything screamed not to?

For an entire year Salaam wrestled with these troubling questions. Gradually the conviction grew that he must follow Jesus. Finally he chose a day to tell Miriam.

That morning, he noticed that Miriam was troubled. She was pacing around their small adobe hut with a look of consternation. He asked, "Miriam, what's wrong?" She began to cry. "O Salaam, I had a dream last night." "Go on," urged Salaam. "I met Jesus in my dream." Miriam hesitated and then continued, "He said, 'Miriam, I love you and I want you to follow me. You must tell Salaam tomorrow. It will be all right.'" Salaam began to cry tears of joy as he told her of his dream a year ago.

From that day Salaam and Miriam have been bold followers of Jesus. They live out their witness by holding hands together in the park in a culture where a woman is expected to walk behind her husband. They sit together on a park bench, causing passersby to ask questions that have led to opportunities to share what Jesus has done in their lives.

The Ancient of Days continues to reveal himself in new and amazing ways. Long ago the prophet Joel prophesied that this would happen: "Your sons and daughters will prophesy, your old men will dream dreams, your young men will see visions. . . . I will pour out my Spirit in those days" (Joel 2:28-29). The apostle Peter also quotes this verse at Pentecost, as the early church experienced the amazing work of the Spirit. So why do we often assume that God has finished working through dreams, visions, and revelations?

As witnesses we are called to obedience—to a person, not to a method. It is obedience to the way of salvation, which is Jesus. Jesus is revealed in God's Word as the way of salvation, and the Holy Spirit testifies to what we know to be true about Jesus. We are called to live out this gospel, even when we cannot fully explain the mystery and wonder of our salvation. You don't need to "figure out" God in order to explain him to others; instead you are called to pursue God in the beauty of his holiness, telling others what you know to be true because God told you through his Word and Spirit.

When you open your heart to God, you are opening to the possibility that God will work in mysterious ways. That can be scary and unfamiliar territory. How do we know what is really from God? Let me offer a few suggestions:

- Any "revelation from God" or prophecy, dream, or vision that contradicts God's Word is not from God. This takes careful, persistent prayer; sometimes what may seem like a contradiction really isn't—remember Peter's vision to kill and eat the "unclean" animals he thought God's Word forbade him to eat?

- We must be careful that we don't rationalize things to fit our liking, because "the heart is deceitful above all things" (Jeremiah 17:9). Our trust is in God's Word and Spirit. He has given us both in full measure to guide us.

- Although God speaks to specific individuals, I believe that God has given his Word and Spirit to be lived out in community. A word of prophecy or vision to an individual is an opportunity to build up the community, according to the mission of God. A community gives balance to such prophecies by "testing" them with the Word of God.

- There is strength in community, but we cannot assume the majority is always right. Remember, Caleb and Joshua were outnumbered and yet they were the only two who were hearing from God.

Find peace in the fact that you will never "figure God out." If you could, you would be God. We can either embrace the mystery of God or erect walls of fear and resistance. I invite you to let the mystery of God have a growing place in your life. Be stretched. Today is a new day. God's Spirit is reaching people in new ways with the original good news. He is inviting you to embrace the mystery and wonder of his witness to the world.

Greedy Little Monkeys

Jesus knew their thoughts and said to them:
"Any kingdom divided against itself will be ruined,
and a house divided against itself will fall."

—Luke 11:17

Monkeys love rice and will do anything to get it. Monkey hunters use this knowledge to capture their prey. They take a coconut and bore a hole in it just big enough for a monkey's little hand. Then they fill the coconut with warm rice and tie it to a tree. Attracted by the smell of the rice, the monkey reaches inside and grabs a handful. Clenched around the rice, the monkey's hand is too big to fit through the hole. For hours the monkey will bang the coconut and try every which way to get the rice out, but it will not let go of its grip on the rice.

Even as the hunter approaches, the monkey will keep a tight grip on the rice. It will be easily captured. What stands between its freedom and its capture is *greed*; its desire to have it all leads to its ultimate destruction.

We are not so different from the greedy little monkeys. We want to have it all, and we want it now. We want to live large, but find ourselves tripping over our affluence. This destructiveness has seeped into the Western church and into our personal witness and walk of faith. Jesus said, "I have come that they may have life, and have it to the full" (John 10:10). How we interpret a "full" life has become the problem. In order to live a full life, we must set our sights on Jesus, "the pioneer and perfecter of faith" (Hebrews 12:2). We need to put Jesus first. We cannot have everything and *then* add Jesus. There simply isn't enough room.

Jesus taught about commitment . . . a lot. Following him requires a singular, healthy, focused commitment. He warned his disciples that it would be easy to get distracted. The tendency of their hearts was to pull in a different direction; to shy away from commitment and pursue self-interests. He sent them out on an evangelistic outreach mission, saying, "Do not take a purse or bag or sandals; and do not greet anyone on the road" (Luke 10:4). Why not? Because he knew they would become distracted. These things are not bad in themselves, but they may be distractions. With so much at stake, a singular vision was required.

Sometimes good things can be a distraction keeping us from the best things. Some of the people Jesus invited to follow him were distracted by other tasks. They wanted to follow Jesus, they said, but first they had more important things to take care of. Jesus replied, "No one who puts his hand to the plow and looks back is fit for service in the kingdom of God" (Luke 9:62).

That seems harsh, but it is a necessary warning. Our lives can become so convoluted with "extras" that we don't even know what we're living for anymore. Suddenly we can find ourselves spending so much time taking care of our stuff that there's no time left to serve others. Or we find our priorities centered on other "important things" and have no time left for Jesus. God knows how quickly our time and heart can get filled with other things, and how difficult it can be for us to extricate ourselves from the pit of pursuing more than God's glory. That is why he makes it clear that we cannot have it all. We cannot serve two masters.

Will it be rice or freedom? We have to choose.

There's a wonderful paradox at work here. When we give up everything to follow Jesus, we find out that he *is* everything. When we seek first Jesus' kingdom and his righteousness, he is our strong tower; he's everything we need. Another important thing that happens when we choose Jesus with this singular focus is this: people notice. Not us, but Jesus. Even if they don't know what they're seeing, they notice Jesus living and working through us. They wonder, "Who is this Jesus that draws this kind of commitment and produces this much joy in a person's life?" And the stage is set for the same transformation we experienced: from "greedy little monkey" to follower of Jesus.

Just Say It!

You who bring good news to Zion, go up on a high mountain.
You who bring good news to Jerusalem, lift up your
voice with a shout, lift it up, do not be afraid;
say to the towns of Judah, "Here is your God!"
—*Isaiah 40:9*

When I was in high school my class put on a benefit concert for a girl who had been injured in a car accident. She'd suffered a head injury that meant she had to relearn how to walk and talk. The benefit was a wonderful celebration of life and community coming together in love to raise money for a wheelchair-accessible van. Various students shared their gifts and talents, and I had the opportunity to speak a few words.

Afterward a young man waited around for the crowd to disburse. Seeing a break in the conversation, he came forward and nervously told me that something I'd said had changed his life. He wanted to know more about Jesus. I froze. Here was an open door—wide open—and I didn't walk through. The young man just stood there. I should have celebrated with him. I should have said something, but I didn't. Was I afraid? I don't think so—I'd just been onstage. Was I unprepared? Probably. What I recall thinking at the time is that I couldn't come up with anything worth saying. My desire to say something profound kept me from giving a "reason for the hope that is within me." I should have just said it.

There are countless reasons why we sometimes drop the ball. Fortunately, our sovereign God is forgiving and graciously presents us with more opportunities for our witness. But that's not an excuse. We need to get better at it. We are called to love people with our service and our very lives (1 Thessalonians 2:8), but sometimes we just need to say it.

I love the story of the seeing man who was blind until he met Jesus. With a little spit and a bold proclamation, Jesus made the man see; as a result, others came to know Jesus that day. The seeing man in the story could have been intimidated by the Pharisees. Instead, he boldly proclaimed his experience with Jesus—not once, but at least twice, under extreme pressure from the Pharisees. He even asked them if they wanted to become Jesus' disciples! What he said wasn't prepared or rehearsed. But it was powerful and it was true.

Peter and John, both uneducated men, also proclaimed boldly what they knew to be true about the crucified and resurrected Christ. They were arrested, imprisoned, and questioned. And still they proclaimed what the Holy Spirit led them to say: "Salvation is found in no one else, for there is no other name given under heaven by which we must be saved" (Acts 4:12). They couldn't help "speaking about what we have seen and heard" (v. 20). They *had* to tell others the good news.

Sometimes we overlook the fact that Jesus proclaimed that he is the only way to the Father (John 14:6). He did this in a pluralistic society where Jews, Romans, Greeks, Medes, Cretans, and others all had very different ideas of what it means to follow God—a society not so different from our own in that respect. But these days more and more Christ followers are having trouble taking a stand like the "seeing man" or like Peter and John. They're reluctant to make exclusive claims about Jesus, or they wonder if it's their "business" to impose their beliefs on others. They seem to believe that the only way we can enjoy harmonious relationships with people is to *not* assert what we believe.

The message about Jesus has not changed. Our mission is not to convince others that we are right, but rather to tell them that God loves us. So let us be wise to listen when the Spirit tells us to listen, and to speak when the Spirit tells us to speak. May our words be accompanied with love and action toward our neighbor.

In the end, you just need to say it. Declare what Jesus has done in your life, and don't apologize. Proclaim the wonderful good news about Jesus, the only one who can bring transformation and hope to broken and "successful" people. If you don't, it's like having the cure to cancer and keeping it to yourself—only magnified.

The Way of Jesus

"Still other seed fell on good soil. It came up, grew and produced a crop, some multiplying thirty, some sixty, some a hundred times."
—Mark 4:8

My third-grade teacher demonstrated an amazing concept to our class. He said if you could work thirty days for someone who would pay you a penny the first day and then double the pay from the previous day every day, you should do it. At first we were skeptical. He drew one cent on the board. Then he multiplied it . . . two cents. He went on doubling to make four, eight, and so on. After a week you'd be up to sixty-four cents for the day. It didn't seem worth it. But right around day 14 things started to get interesting—you'd make $81.92. With sixteen days to go! By the end of the demonstration we were convinced. On day 30 the pay would be $5,368,709.12, with a grand total of $10,737,418.23 for the thirty days. Multiplication was definitely the way to go!

Jesus also knew that multiplication was the way to go. It was his way of making disciples. In the parable of the sower, he explained that if the seed of the gospel is planted in someone who hears the word and accepts it, that person will "produce a crop—some thirty, some sixty, some a hundred times what was sown" (Mark 4:20). That is the beauty of multiplication. The Holy Spirit has planted the good news in our hearts and is cultivating that good news in our lives in order to reproduce it in others. This was the way of Jesus.

Jesus embodied the Father's will and carried it out by relying on the Holy Spirit. If we want to know God's will, we should look to Jesus. Jesus spent his life showing the way, giving his disciples a clear picture of how he multiplied disciples and how we are to multiply disciples today.

- First, Jesus invited his disciples to "come and see." This was step 1—the *show* stage. Jesus' miracle at Cana and his many other demonstrations of power and interactions with people *showed* his followers what he wanted to teach them.

- Step 2 was the *join* stage. Jesus encouraged his disciples to "come alongside." He included them in his ministry and allowed them to practice under his careful direction. At the feeding of the five thousand, Jesus said to his disciples, "You give them something to eat." We learn by doing.

- Next the Master gave opportunity for his disciples to "fly solo." This was step 3—the *solo* stage. "You do it, I'll watch." He expected the disciples to model his teaching throughout the day. This wasn't some part-time gig. It was a committed lifestyle to love people completely . . . Jesus' way. One day the disciples came back to Jesus a little frustrated: they didn't understand why they couldn't cast out a particular demon. Jesus patiently provided instruction: this particular demon could only be cast out with much prayer and fasting. Jesus pushed his disciples to step out in faith under his steady guidance. They learned that even when they were "flying solo," they were never truly alone.

- Step 4 was sending the disciples out into the world to "go and be"—the *go* stage. Jesus gave them everything they needed to be successful, including the presence and power of the Holy Spirit. Jesus sent them out with instructions to be his witnesses and demonstrate his way in "all the world." This assignment was bigger than they expected, and their witness was more powerful than they could imagine.

- The final step in Jesus' instructions for multiplying disciples was to "go and make disciples," bringing the process full circle back to the *show* stage. The way of Jesus was to multiply himself through his disciples. He reminded them once again what they must do in order to make other disciples: bring people to *identify with the powerful rule and reign of God* on earth (symbolized with baptism), *teach them to obey everything he taught*, and *continue this lifelong work in his strength*.

Sometimes we're too content with addition when God is calling us to multiply. There was a man who preached to sparse crowds on a routine basis. Discouraged, he thought about giving up his ministry. One day, after preaching to another slim crowd, a few people came to know Jesus for the first time. What he never knew was that one of the men who came to Jesus that night was Billy Graham, who would go on to become one of the greatest evangelists of our time!

We serve a God of multiplication. Our Savior taught a multiplying way of discipleship. His Spirit continues to work through us in a multiplying effort. Consider living a life of multiplication, not addition. With this minor but important shift, you will begin following the way of Jesus.

Yardstick

"Give, and it will be given to you. A good measure, pressed down, shaken together and running over, will be poured into your lap. For with the measure you use, it will be measured to you."
—*Luke 6:38*

"That didn't count." "Did too!" "Did not!" I remember counting to one hundred very quickly if I was "it" for hide and seek. If I'd find the others too quickly, a debate would ensue. We all want a measuring stick for what's fair. It gives us the boundaries and context we need to understand whether we're accomplishing what we set out to do.

It's been said of powerful people that they carry "a big stick." One such person, who happened to be one of my teachers, always carried a yardstick. This yardstick was her best friend. She ate with it, walked with it, and quite frequently used it on our desks. She never struck anyone with it, but when she hit my desk—if I happened to be checking on a very important issue with my neighbor—it certainly got my attention.

God uses measurement in many different ways throughout Scripture, our measure for faith and life. God gives us the *yardstick* of his law, a gift that gives us freedom within his boundaries for our lives. God *counts* people and knows each by name. God *weighs* the heart of Balshazzar and finds it lacking. Armies are counted, and sometimes limited, so that *God's* power and might are on display. God *measures* how we should worship him with detailed instructions for building the tabernacle and temple, and ultimately with instructions from Jesus to worship him in Spirit and in truth. The new city in John's Revelation is measured with a rod; its vastness is equal to the entire known world at the time.

God cares about measurement, outlining our good and his glory. Yet somewhere along the way we slipped away from God's yardstick and began using our own. Today we'll look at three key measures of our witness: the measure of our call, the measure of our love, and the measure of success.

First, our call. Jesus tells us to count the cost of following him, including the difficulties we should expect along the way. Many have given their lives for the sake of this call. In fact, this past century has had more martyrs for Jesus than all of the past centuries combined. Many times we are eager to serve Jesus on our own terms. But what will be our witness when our comfort and freedom disappear?

My friend in Kyrgyzstan told me of a Scandinavian family who had measured the cost of their witness. Responding to God's call to minister to the "Kyrgie" people, this family tried to sell their home and their large sheep farm, but there were no takers. They prayed that someone would come and take care of their flock, which had been in the family for many generations, but no one came. The man said, "I had a decision to make: should we stay and care for this flock that had become an extension of our family, or did God have sheep in other pastures that we must care for?" What did they do? "We had to have them slaughtered," the man said. "We had to follow God."

Next we'll look at the measure of our love. Peter asked Jesus, "How many times am I supposed to forgive someone—seven times?" "No," Jesus replied. "Seventy times seven." We're supposed to show others an unlimited measure of grace and forgiveness—not just the ones who are kind to us, but everyone (Luke 6:32-34). This includes a preempted graciousness in which we give people the benefit of the doubt and assume the best instead of the worst. That doesn't mean we throw out our measure of right and wrong, but that we're quicker to show grace than impose judgment. A friend of mine once said, "People are eager to judge themselves according to their own best intentions and judge others according to their worst actions." Our ability to extend grace is directly tied to the measure of love we have toward others, which God can (and will) increase.

Third, we'll look at the measure of success. The religious leaders of Jesus' day had a way of measuring what they thought devoted followers of God should look like and how they should act. Jesus changed all that. He altered and raised the standard, telling the disciples how hard it is to enter the kingdom using their measure of success.

The man who came to Jesus had it all going for him. He was an impeccably moral man who closely followed the law and became very wealthy—which was thought a sure measure of God's blessing. Then Jesus started talking about camels going through the eye of needles, causing a stir of fear among the disciples: "Who then can be saved?" (Matthew 19:25). Jesus comforted their hearts by assuring them that with God, "everything is possible." Jesus was the new yardstick, full of grace and truth.

How do we measure our success as a witness? We cannot measure effectiveness with conversions or baptisms alone, but also with obedient conversations and seeds planted. Witnesses often look different than the polished and neat appearances of our traditional expectations. People live successfully under the yardstick of God, a measurement we may not expect, yet do well to emulate.

Discussion Guide

Opening *(5-10 minutes)*

Take turns briefly sharing something that stood out from this week's readings. Don't discuss them; just mention them for now.

Then have someone read the following focus statement out loud:

What Jesus tells us about the kingdom is often counterintuitive. He tells us to seek first the kingdom and his righteousness, and then everything else will be added as well; we want to add the kingdom to everything else. The kingdom cannot be found unless we give up our way of finding, our way of thinking, our way of being. We must surrender in order to have victory. When we recognize our need and our naked dependence on God, we are blessed with the presence and power of the Holy Spirit. Only then can we carry out God's kingdom work. This is a new way of thinking—a great reversal.

Bible Study *(15-20 minutes)*

The following Scripture passages are examples of "great reversals." Read each one, and then "unpack" the significance of each for our own life and witness:

- Luke 17:33

- 1 Corinthians 1:19, 21

- 2 Corinthians 12:9-10

- 1 Peter 5:5

- Luke 14:11

Activity Variation
Divide the texts above among the group and briefly report back to each other.

Read the following passages and answer the questions below.

- Ezekiel 44:25-27; Luke 10:25-37
  Keep in mind that the priests and Levites who passed by "on the other side" of the Samaritan did so to follow the law. How does this further highlight Jesus' story and what he desires from us?

- Matthew 5:17
  How does this "new way of thinking"—this counterintuitive "great reversal"—square with the Law, according to Jesus?

Discussion *(15-20 minutes)*

1. "The Ancient of Days continues to reveal himself in new and amazing ways" (Day 1). What are some of the ways God continues to reveal himself to you? To the body of Christ as a whole?

2. Identify one or more things that have become the "rice" in your life (see Day 2). What steps can you take to release the grip you have on it (or it has on you)?

3. "How beautiful on the mountains are the feet of those who bring good news" (Isaiah 52:7). Before your feet can be "beautiful," your mind and heart need to get there first. What are some of the places and people in your life that need to hear the good news?

4. God is not counting on you to reach a specific number of people, just consistent obedience to teach and reach a few. How does that encourage you in your witness?

5. Often modern religious leaders use their own scorecard to measure the success of their ministry. How have you measured "success" as a Christian witness in your life? How might this measure need to change in order to be in line with God's yardstick?

Activity Variation
Instead of using the questions above, go back to the comments people made in the Opening time of your session about this week's readings. Take time to discuss them and raise questions of your own.

Closing *(5-10 minutes)*

Spend a few minutes sharing joys and concerns that have come up this past week. Then pray together for these items. Close your prayer by reading the following in unison:

> Thank you, Father, for showing us a different way according to your Son, Jesus. We praise you for his sacrificial death and for his resurrection. Help us to be the people you are calling us to be. Deepen our surrender to your will. Fill us with your presence and power. Enfold us into your kingdom work. And may we love the way you love, even when it's easier to walk away. Amen.

Activity Variation

Pray as suggested above, but instead of praying with the whole group, find a partner and pray with him or her.

Action Options

Group: Share stories of your childhood with the group. Focus on childhood assumptions you made about God and the way God works that changed when you got older. Spend time reflecting on your current assumptions that may need refining. Perhaps you have been challenged by people on several occasions or have encountered an issue several times, and now is the time to deal with it. Listen and encourage one another to allow the Holy Spirit to cut through personal assumptions and uncover God's truth, both individually and as a group.

Personal: Most battles to live like Jesus or live for oneself begin in our minds. This week do two things:

- Whenever you have a consuming thought contrary to God's will—a stab that forms at the base of your neck and threatens to flow out on your tongue—say out loud, "My mind is yours, Jesus," and allow him to take over.

- Go up to someone you normally wouldn't talk to because they're "different" than you, and express an encouraging word. Get out of your "zone" and create new space for the Spirit to roam in your life.

In Every Sphere

The Great Wooer

*The Lord is not slow in keeping his promise, as some understand
slowness. Instead he is patient with you, not wanting
anyone to perish, but everyone to come to repentance.*

—2 Peter 3:9

*"I, when I am lifted up from the earth,
will draw all people to myself."*

—John 12:32

The shopping plaza was busy that day. My two-and-a-half-
year-old daughter, Ally, was right by my side as we made
our way through the racks of merchandise. As I stopped
for a moment to talk with a friend, I was conscious of a few
children playing around our feet. Then I looked down. Ally
was gone.

Fear rose up like bile in my throat. How could I have lost
her? She was right there a second ago. I pushed through the
crowd, searching, searching everywhere but couldn't find her.
Minutes seemed like hours as others joined the search. Just
as my heart was about to burst, I saw her. She was chasing a

grasshopper through the marketplace with not a care in the world. I wrapped her in my arms and promised myself I'd never let go again. I would do anything to keep her safe.

Most parents experience this heart-stopping terror at some point. I believe God must feel a similar terror when his children stray away from him. The God revealed in Scripture would do anything to find his lost children. He desperately seeks to love those who are far from him. "Desperate?" you may be wondering. "Can the all-powerful God really be desperate?" I don't know how else to describe a God who sent his only Son to die in order to bring us back to him. That's desperate love.

It began in a garden. Adam and Eve were living in perfect harmony with the rest of creation, with each other, and with God—until that fateful day when they tangled with the serpent. Afterward they ran away—no longer innocent but guilty and ashamed. God ran too. God ran toward them and called out, "Where are you?" Didn't God already know where they were? Of course, and that is why he desperately needed to find them. Adam and Eve needed God. More than they knew, they needed him.

God found them and loved them. And this is how God showed his love: "He sent his one and only Son into the world that we might live through him" (1 John 4:9). God provided a way for all people to find him by sending Jesus to find everyone (Joel 2:32; Acts 2:21; Romans 10:13). Jesus came to seek and save the lost (which is all of us), and the Father continues to pursue those who are separated from him with a desperate love that will not fail. God began his pursuit in the garden with the question, "Where are you?" and God will continue his pursuit until it's complete.

Because God is love he is also the great Wooer, calling people to himself with the enduring love of a good father. God is asking us to have eyes for the world as he does. So what does that mean? What might that look like for our witness? It is nothing less than a comprehensive and complete demonstration of God's love for people.

This is a profoundly simple concept, but one that is infinitely difficult to unfold through our lives. We need to ask ourselves, "How much do I care about other people? How am I demonstrating that love in my life?" It's not about the wonderful programs in your church, although some of those may be excellent ways to demonstrate God's love. And it's not about convincing people that they're supposed to follow some new moral standard. Put simply, it's loving people for who they are—children of the Father—and where they are—with different degrees of certainty about the Father's love.

God loves all of his children that way. He loves you that way. To understand God's heart for his children and our role in demonstrating his love is to "try to persuade people" to accept this truth (2 Corinthians 5:11)—to woo them.

The Least

"Truly I tell you, whatever you did for one of the least
of these brothers and sisters of mine, you did for me."
—*Matthew 25:40*

Jonah was on a dangerous mission . . . running away from God. You know the story: minor prophet, escape cruise, big storm, major fish, dry land . . . Now fast-forward to the other part of the story, where Jonah proclaims God's Word to those unbelieving Ninevites. After such a harrowing ordeal, you'd think Jonah would have learned his lesson. Instead Jonah's so angry at God for sparing those Ninevites that he wants to take his own life when they repent and believe.

The disciples were on a dangerous mission . . . in the path of God. You know this story too: Jesus talking, children crowding, disciples shooing, Jesus angry, love shared, children blessed: "Let the little children come to me . . . for the kingdom of heaven belongs to such as these" (Matthew 19:14). After Jesus' example, you'd think the disciples would understand the need to care for "the least." You'd think they'd get it. Instead they argue about who will be greatest in Jesus' kingdom. During their final hours with Jesus, the disciples didn't want to betray Jesus—a chorus of "Is it I, Lord?" echoed around the supper table. But neither did they want to perform the menial task of washing each other's feet.

I share these negative examples because these were real people with real issues . . . not so different from you and me. It's the natural pattern of our hearts to want to be more significant than others. To believe that we have it right and others are wrong. It's natural for us to try to associate with the important people and hope to gain somehow from this association. That's been happening ever since sin entered the world. It's the root of racism, sexism, and all the other forms of exclusion we practice. It's the part of us that's still steeped in sin, waiting to be redeemed by the transformative power of Jesus. As a result, we overlook, bypass, and perhaps even shun "the least." Single mothers and fathers, homeless people, orphans, minorities, refugees, those who have physical or mental disabilities, and people who are poor and uneducated are second-class citizens in the eyes of the world and even in our pews.

People who love God are called to love and care for others—the greatest and especially "the least." Those of us who live in homes where the garages are bigger than the homes of many of the world's poor people need to be reminded of this.

I believe our witness extends to leveraging our affluence to conquer poverty. "From everyone who has been given much, much will be demanded" (Luke 12:48). This starts with the deep conviction that we're supposed to make a difference. "There will always be poor people in the land," we read in Deuteronomy 15:11. But a few verses earlier, it says, "There need be no poor people among you" (v. 4). One thing that distinguishes a godly society from an ungodly one is not giving up on "the least." Even when it's easier to give up on a seemingly endless, unsolvable task, God calls us to remain steadfast in our witness.

So important is our witness to "the least" that Jesus equates it with loving and caring for Jesus himself (Matthew 25:40).

So important is concern for the poor that the prophet Ezekiel includes neglecting the poor and needy in the same breath as the "detestable practices," the sexual sins and depravity of Sodom: "'Now this was the sin of your sister Sodom: She and her daughters were arrogant, overfed and unconcerned; they did not help the poor and needy'" (Ezekiel 16:47-49).

The sins of Sodom were multiple, but Scripture highlights the arrogant neglect of the poor as the main one. God completely destroyed this city because it went against his heart—his concern for "the least." Through the Spirit's power, may our witness encompass those who are "the least" in the eyes of the world, for the kingdom of God belongs to them.

Iwo Jima

Though the fig tree does not bud and there are no grapes on the vines, though the olive crop fails and the fields produce no food, though there are no sheep in the pen and no cattle in the stalls, yet I will rejoice in the LORD, I will be joyful in God my Savior.
—Habbakuk 3:17-18

"Remember what I told you: 'Servants are not greater than their master.' If they persecuted me, they will persecute you also."
—John 15:20

An armada of American ships charged toward the Japanese island of Iwo Jima in February 1945. Aboard the ships were 70,647 United States Marines. Boys mostly, averaging in age between seventeen and nineteen, they had only trained about a year for the coming battle. They would make an amphibious landing on the black beaches of this tiny Pacific island 660 miles south of Tokyo.

As this speck of land came into view, the men would have noticed a "mountain" on its southern end. You couldn't miss it. Rising more than five hundred feet from the crashing waves below, this mountain had become a fortress for the embedded Japanese army. Dug in and heavily armed, the Japanese waited for the invading force.

Allied forces had already experienced deadly encounters with Japanese soldiers on Guam, Saipan, and many other Pacific islands. But they knew Iwo Jima would be significantly worse. *This* piece of rocky, windswept land, totaling eight square miles, was special to the Japanese emperor and his people. *This* island was actually part of Japan. No foreign invader had set foot on Japanese soil in thousands of years.

Iwo Jima, as the Marines soon learned, would be a fight to the death.

The apostle Paul would have understood the men charging the shores of Iwo Jima. He encountered his own Iwo Jima as he tried to present the gospel to people who would rather live life for themselves: he was "hard pressed . . . , persecuted . . . , struck down . . ." (2 Corinthians 4:8-12). Paul faced persecution from the Pharisees, who wanted to control their experience with God, and from pagans, who wanted a life of pleasure instead of obedience. He understood that his mission was a fight to the death—and that it had greater consequences than physical death. This was a fight for people's souls. In spite of the cost, Paul continued to share the good news of Jesus, the One who rescues us from a life corrupted by sin and destined for destruction (Romans 7:24).

We honor the men of Iwo Jima for their sacrifice. They recognized the battle and the obstacles ahead of them. They understood the cost and stormed the beaches. But what life could have greater meaning than a life of sacrifice, dedicated to winning the souls of others?

It can be very difficult to love others. Some people can be downright ornery and cantankerous; it would take an act of God to get a smile. But they are the very ones we're called to love. "If you love those who love you, what credit is that to you?" Jesus says. "Even sinners love those who love them" (Luke 6:32-34).

Jesus tells us to count the cost (Luke 14:28), as did the men of Iwo Jima and the apostle Paul. Living as his disciples *will* have a cost. But he never calls us to do what he is not willing to do himself. His grace will keep you wherever his call leads you. You may encounter resistance that's painful and downright messy, causing you to sometimes question whether it's worth it.

We need to recognize the battle before us, count the cost, and storm the beaches for the souls of our friends and neighbors. It's what our King would do. . . . It's what our King did.

All the People on the Ball

*"And this gospel of the kingdom will be preached in the whole world
as a testimony to all nations, and then the end will come."*
—Matthew 24:14

"Red and yellow, black and white, they are precious in his sight; Jesus loves the little children of the world." So sang my five-year-old daughter. And then she said, "I love all the people on the ball, Daddy." How about you? Do you love all the people on the ball?

It's estimated that there are 13,511 known languages (with 30,000 dialects) in the world, among 12,000 to 16,000 different people groups. About 2,238 languages have at least a portion of Scripture translated—so there's plenty of work to do. But when people go out into the far corners of the earth to share the gospel, something happens that goes beyond translation. Their lives show that they care about "all the people on the ball." God is calling us to reach people of every tribe and ethnic group—whether they're across the globe or part of the surging immigration population at our own back door—for his glory. How are we to love all those people?

Jesus sets the example. He goes where no one else wants to go, repeatedly challenging the religious system by telling stories and parables that lift up those who are cast aside by the rest of society. Take the Samaritans. Everyone "knew" they were half-breed traitors, but Jesus told a story in which the Samaritan was the only good guy. He hung out with a Samaritan woman, even sharing her cup, a definite no-no for at least two reasons: she was a Samaritan and she was a woman. And then there was the Decapolis—an area of ten cities—where all the "pagan" people lived. Jesus and his disciples frequently spent time with them. His neighbors wondered why Jesus had to visit those pagan people in Phoenicia and Syria. Couldn't he leave well enough alone? Jesus did these things because he loves "all the people on the ball." In fact, he died for them.

As witnesses of Jesus, are we willing to follow? Are we willing to change our paths so that we come in contact with people who aren't like us? Are we willing to be reconciled to people of other races or ethnic groups? Reconciliation with each other goes hand in hand with reconciliation with God: "Those who love God must also love one another" (1 John 4:21). Without being in relationship with others, the chance for reconciliation is slim. We can't be content with loving all the people on the ball from a distance. This can be frightening and uncomfortable at first. People are a lot like porcupines. We can't get too close to one another without poking each other. Sometimes we might bleed a little in a lot of places. But in Jesus, reconciliation is possible. He has removed our "quills" and taken them upon himself (2 Corinthians 5:21).

It always disturbs me that Sunday morning is the most segregated hour of the week in America. How does a world that is far from Jesus be reconciled to him if the church doesn't lead the way? Too often we distance ourselves from the people with whom we need to be reconciled. We naturally pull away from diversity and gravitate toward sameness. It's the story of Babel all over again. Our churches should look like the neighbor-hoods around them if we're really obeying Jesus' command to "go into all the world." Loving all the people on the ball means our witness must encompass people with different ethnicities, social classes, genders, and political persuasions.

Legal slavery is gone, but the ugly legacy of racism persists from generation to generation. The power and prejudice of the majority continues to alienate those from minority ethnic groups. That is why more than ever we must courage-ously look for opportunities to be reconciled with one an-other, extending God's grace in various forms: repentance, forgiveness, listening without being defensive, and going be-yond whatever is required to understand and love each other. If we don't do that, we all lose.

One flip through the channels confirms America's fascina-tion with politics. Has our witness slid into an agenda that runs Jesus' agenda alongside the vein of our culture? Would you be disappointed if Jesus voted Democratic or Republican? With-out even realizing it, our witness can become so fused with a political or cultural agenda that the bubble in which we live just keeps getting bigger, and hope for reconciliation floats fur-ther away.

It is helpful to take a deliberate step back from our own cul-ture and honestly assess where we are. This is difficult to do, and that is why we need to invite people from other cultures into this exercise and listen to each other. Because "all people" means *all* people. Like Jesus, we're supposed to love all the people on the ball.

This Means War

*Put on the full armor of God, so that you can take your
stand against the devil's schemes. For our struggle is not
against flesh and blood, but against the rulers, against the
authorities, against the powers of this dark world and against
the spiritual forces of evil in the heavenly realms.*
—Ephesians 6:11-12

I t was cold outside. The bitter chill created by wind and white
stuff threatened to rob their bodies of all heat. But out they
went, these brave little souls of winter, too distracted by visions of the grandeur outside to be fazed by the cold.

What I've found laborious is the extensive preparation kids
require before they step into the arctic world. Sometimes we
spend as much time getting them ready as they do playing
outside. Strategic layers are necessary to form a hermetic seal,
keeping the cold from penetrating to the skin: socks over pants,
snow pants over boots, and always gloves first, then the coat.
It's like getting "armored up" for battle against a cold enemy
that can't be seen but is out there all the same.

Just as a child is often unaware of the damage severe cold can do to the skin, we are often unaware of the extensive harm that can result when we don't prepare for the war that is waged in the spiritual realm. This passage from Ephesians calls us to recognize that we're in a battle against "the devil's schemes" so that we can put on "the full armor of God" and come out swinging. What we do or say and how we pray greatly affect the spiritual battle that is waging for the hearts, minds, and souls of God's children.

No wonder Jesus tells us to love the Lord our God with all our heart, soul, mind, and strength. In loving God so completely, we dedicate every part of ourselves to his service. This posture is the foundational way we put on God's armor rather than relying on our own rusty set.

Jesus often refers to our actions stirring heavenly consequences. When a lost son sees the error of his ways and comes home, his father throws him a huge party and heaven rejoices (Luke15). When a young man asks Jesus what good thing he must do to be saved, Jesus tells him to sell all his possessions and give the money to the poor in order to store up treasures in heaven (Matthew 19:21). With these stories, Jesus is teaching us that there's more going on than meets the eye.

The same is true of our witness in this world: what we do and say has an impact in the realm of spiritual warfare. Preparation and prayer are essential. In order to follow God's leading, we're called to "test the spirits to see whether they are from God" (1 John 4:1). Prayer is an essential part of testing the spirits and discerning how God is leading us. We need to understand how much we depend on God's power in our lives, "for in him we live and move and have our being" (Acts 17:28). Our witness against the spiritual forces of evil happens "not by might nor by power, but by [God's] Spirit" (Zechariah 4:6).

The warfare we engage in as witnesses of Jesus happens primarily on our knees. Without the weapon of prayer, even our physical acts of service and words of proclamation fall flat. Prayer is one of the greatest offensive weapons we have been given. The

Spirit uses prayer to alter our lives and the lives of others for the glory of the King. It reaches far beyond our own five senses and opens a conduit for heaven to come down to earth.

We're in a war. But even though the devil is still scheming and the battles are still raging, the outcome of the war is certain. God wins! *We win!*

Discussion Guide

Opening *(5-10 minutes)*

Where is the scariest place you've ever been? How about the safest place? Take turns briefly mentioning the places that come to mind around these extremes and what made each place scary or safe.

Then have someone read the following focus statement out loud:

> Right before Jesus ascended into heaven he told his disciples to go "into all the world"—into every sphere and every nook and cranny of every heart. He wanted this to be an all-out, all-hands-on-deck rescue mission for those who were far away from his Father. Jesus is calling us to be involved in every area of the world, including government, education, media, economy, entertainment, and every other industry. God has placed his body, the church, in various contexts to carry out the work of the King. Our worship of God means focusing our hearts on his kingdom, which he has chosen to reveal in our lives.

Bible Study *(20 minutes)*

Read the following passages and then discuss the questions below each.

- John 18:1-9; Exodus 13:4; John 8:58
  Notice especially verse 6 of John 18. What is going on here? How does this relate to God's declaration in Exodus 3:14 and John 8:58?

- Philippians 2:9-13
  This passage talks about the reality that "every tongue [will] acknowledge that Jesus Christ is Lord." How does this reflect God's sovereignty? How should we respond to this reality? How should it affect the way we reach out to the world?

- John 14:12
  What does Jesus mean that "all who have faith in [him] . . . will do even greater things"? In what way has the church done even greater things? What greater things are still to come?

  Why is the "because" in this verse so vitally important? What person is it related to? (If you're stuck, read John 16:7.)

- 1 John 1:1-4
  What have you seen or heard lately in your life that others need to hear? Who might you tell this to?

  If you can't think of anything, is it because you have nothing to tell or that you haven't noticed? Or that you have no one to tell it to in the pattern you're in? Honesty here is freeing . . . this is a place to start fresh.

- Acts 17:17
  To whom is God calling you to witness?

Discussion *(15-20 minutes)*

1. God cannot help but to seek his children with a desperate love—it's an unchangeable part of his character. Often we use the word "desperation" in a situation that seems hopeless. Since God cannot fail, how does his character demonstrate a holy desperation to save his children?

2. "Even when it's easier to give up on a seemingly endless, unsolvable task, God calls us to remain steadfast in our witness" (Day 2). What is our responsibility to "the least" in our neighborhood? In our country? In the world? Why is our witness to these people so important?

3. The heart of God is a deep desire that no one is lost (2 Peter 3:9). What things can keep us from recognizing the seriousness of the battle for lost souls in our lives? Are we on a path of pursuing a goal worth dying for?

4. "Reconciliation with each other goes hand in hand with reconciliation with God" (Day 4). What are some ways we might intentionally place ourselves in the path of forming new friendships outside our normal ethnic, social, or political sphere? What does that have to do with our witness to "all people"?

5. How have you experienced spiritual warfare in your life? How does "putting on the full armor of God" help us withstand the power of evil in the world and advance the reign of God on earth?

Closing *(5-10 minutes)*

Spend a few minutes sharing joys and concerns you'd like to have the group pray for. Then spend time in prayer. You may want to use the following sentence starters to structure your prayer, pausing after each to allow group members to add to the prayer, either silently or out loud:

Gracious God, thank you for your work in our lives this past week, especially in the joys and concerns we have mentioned here . . .

Holy Spirit, open our hearts so that we may hear and see clearly your call in the coming week . . .

Risen Lord, in your name we renounce our fears. Help us to share freely what we have seen and heard you doing in our lives. Help us to love others the way you love us . . .

Amen.

Alternate Approach

After sharing joys and concerns with each other, spend some time in prayer, closing by reading the following prayer out loud:

From the ends of the earth, from the depths of the sea, from the heights of the heavens, your name is to be praised. Lord, we remember your love and faithfulness to us this week. You have called us to the ends of the earth, but sometimes our heart grows weary and faint. Forgive us, and lead us by your Spirit in the way of Jesus. Our hope is in you. Thank you for the unfolding reality of your rule and reign over all the earth. We give you all the praise and glory. Amen.

Action Options

Look at the options below, and choose at least one of the suggestions for following up this week's session, either as a group or individually.

Group: Brainstorm some ways your group could respond to God's call to share the good news. Here are a couple of ideas:

- Consider visiting a homeless shelter together. Don't just serve, but spend time talking to the people you meet.

- Write letters to your political representative on behalf of an organization that seeks justice for "the least," such as Bread for the World.

- Write notes of encouragement to the missionaries your church supports.

Then choose one of the ideas and set aside a time to carry it out.

Personal: Choose one of the following options:

Option 1

Our witness begins with small things. This week perform one act of intentional, sacrificial service for someone you know—something that inconveniences you or makes you go out of your way for that person.

Option 2

Do something for God you've never done before. Don't worry about particular giftedness—just listen to where God is calling you to expand your obedience. Perhaps you could visit a local ministry and see where they need help on your lunch break. Or write to a missionary and ask for specific ways you can help support his or her mission with your prayers and other resources.

Option 3

Open up your heart to the possibility that God may want to send you to the ends of the earth or to invest more fully as an agent of transformation in your own neighborhood. Ask God where he wants you to go as you seek to love the world.

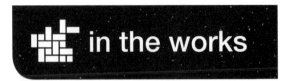
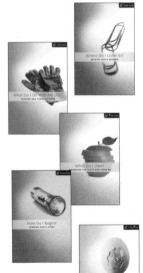